# BOOK A

# Spanish Is Fun

# BOOK A

# Spanish Is Fun

## Lively Lessons for Beginners

**Heywood Wald, PhD**
Martin Van Buren High School
New York City

When ordering this book, please specify *either* **R 448 W**
*or* SPANISH IS FUN, BOOK A

Dedicated to serving

**AMSCO**

*our nation's youth*

**AMSCO SCHOOL PUBLICATIONS, INC.**
**315 Hudson Street/New York, N.Y. 10013**

**Illustrations by Ed Malsberg**

ISBN 0-87720-531-0

# Preface

SPANISH IS FUN, BOOK A offers an introductory program that makes communication in Spanish a natural, personalized, enjoyable, and rewarding experience. The book provides all the elements for an introductory-level course.

SPANISH IS FUN, BOOK A helps students learn communicative skills through simple materials in visually focused contexts. Students can easily relate these contexts to their own experiences. Easy-to-answer questions require students to speak about their daily lives, express their opinions, and supply real information. Topic-based lessons dealing with functional situations are designed to develop proficiency in listening, speaking, reading, and writing. Cultural connections are built into the various lesson components.

SPANISH IS FUN, BOOK A consists of five parts. Each part contains four lessons, followed by a **Repaso,** in which vocabulary and structure are recapitulated and practiced through a variety of **actividades** that include games and puzzles as well as more conventional types of exercises. Lessons 12 and 20 are each followed by an Achievement Test.

Each lesson includes a step-by-step sequence of student-directed elements designed to make the materials immediately accessible, encourage communication and self-expression, and give students the feeling that they can have fun learning Spanish.

## Vocabulary

Each lesson begins with topically related sets of drawings that convey the meanings of new words in Spanish without recourse to English. This device enables students to make a direct and vivid association between the Spanish terms and their meanings. The vocabulary sets are followed by **actividades** that also use picture stimuli to practice and review Spanish words and expressions.

To facilitate comprehension, the book uses cognates of English words wherever suitable, especially in Lesson 1, which is based entirely on Spanish words that are identical to or closely resemble their English equivalents. Beginning the course in this way shows students that Spanish is not so "foreign" after all and helps them overcome any fears that they may have about learning a foreign language.

## Structures

SPANISH IS FUN, BOOK A uses a simple, straightforward presentation of new structural elements. These elements are introduced in small learning components—one at a time—and are directly followed by appropriate **actividades,** many of them visually cued and personalized. The text guides students into making their own discoveries and formulating their own conclusions about structures. Thus, students gain a feeling of accomplishment and success.

## Reading

Each lesson contains a short, entertaining narrative or playlet that features the new vocabulary and structural elements and reinforces previously learned expressions and grammar. These passages deal with topics that are related to the everyday experiences of today's student generation. Cognates and near-cognates are used extensively.

## Conversation

Short situational dialogs—sometimes practical, sometimes humorous—provide models for meaningful communication in all lessons beginning with Lesson 2. All conversations are illustrated to provide a sense of realism. They are accompanied by illustrated dialog exercises that serve as springboards for personalized conversation.

## Testing

The two Achievement Tests are designed to give *all* students a sense of accomplishment. The tests use a variety of techniques through which comprehension of structure and vocabulary as well as situational skills may be evaluated. Teachers may use the Achievement Tests as they appear in the book or modify them to fit particular needs.

A separate *Teacher's Manual and Key,* available from the publisher, provides suggestions for teaching all elements in SPANISH IS FUN, BOOK A, additional practice and testing materials, and a complete key to all exercises and puzzles.

The Author

# Contents

# Primera

## Parte

# 1 El español—una lengua importante

## Words That Are the Same or Similar in Spanish and English; How to Say "The" in Spanish

Suppose someone offered you a free ticket—a ticket that would allow you to travel to wonderful lands hundreds or even thousands of miles away. Some of these lands would be tropical islands with white, sandy beaches and swaying palm trees surrounded by crystal clear waters. Others would be mountainous lands with towering peaks reaching into the clouds and cities so high that their climate is an eternal springtime. Still others would be modern industrial countries with factories, bustling seaports, and cities teeming with millions of people. Of course, anyone with a spirit of adventure would be overjoyed at taking such a thrilling voyage.

These countries are not fantasies; they do exist. They are countries in Europe, South and Central America, the Caribbean, and our immediate neighbor to the South, Mexico. Many of you will probably visit these countries someday, and your trip will be a wonderful experience.

Of course, the people who live in these lands do not speak English. They speak Spanish. So, if you want to communicate with them, you will have to learn Spanish.

But, don't worry. Learning Spanish won't be hard at all. In fact, you're going to have a terrific time doing it, and this book will help you along. As you go through the book, lesson by lesson, learning the new material, you will soon be able to say common, everyday expressions, recognize names of different foods, ask directions, use numbers, tell time, give and receive information, go shopping, and, in general, get along in Spanish.

3

Each lesson contains lots of useful words and loads of activities that are different, exciting, and fun to do. There are hundreds of colorful pictures to help you, so that you will be able to think in Spanish without having to go back to English.

So what are we waiting for? Let's begin! Welcome to the Spanish language!

**1** There are lots of words that are the same in Spanish and in English. Pronounce them in the Spanish way. Your teacher will show you how:

| | | |
|---|---|---|
| el actor | el doctor | el piano |
| el animal | el dragón | popular |
| el auto | el general | el taxi |
| el cereal | el hospital | terrible |
| el chocolate | el hotel | la televisión |
| el color | horrible | tropical |

**2** Here are some words that look just a little different from English:

| | | |
|---|---|---|
| la actriz | el camello | el insecto |
| americano | el diccionario | inteligente |
| el apartamento | la familia | la medicina |
| el automóvil | famoso | la música |
| el barbero | la fotografía | plástico |
| la bicicleta | la fruta | la princesa |
| el calendario | importante | la rosa |

**3** Here are some words that are different from English. Try to figure out their meanings:

| | | |
|---|---|---|
| el aeropuerto | el estudiante | la lámpara |
| el banco | la fiesta | el parque |
| el café | la flor | el teatro |
| el cine | el gigante | el tren |

**4** Lección 1

**4** And, finally, here are some words that don't look at all like English. Try to figure out what they mean by the pictures:

the man

**el hombre**

the woman

**la mujer**

**el niño**

the boy

**la niña**

the girl

El español—una lengua importante    **5**

the house

**la casa**

the record

**el disco**

the chicken

**el pollo**

the book

**el libro**

the father

**el padre**

the mother

**la madre**

the cat
**el gato**

the dog
**el perro**

*the friend (mas.)*

**el amigo**

*the friend (fem.)*

**la amiga**

*the school*

**la escuela**

*the young lady; miss*

**la señorita**

*the pen*

**la pluma**

**el periódico**

*the newspaper*

**la iglesia**

*the church*

El español—una lengua importante

**5** Now let's look at another difference between Spanish and English.

Did you notice the words **el** and **la** before all of the nouns? These two words are Spanish words for "the." That's right. Spanish has two words for "the" in the singular: **el** and **la**. The word **el** is used before masculine nouns and **la** is used before feminine nouns.

How do we know which words are masculine and which are feminine? With some words it's easy. Obviously, **madre** (*mother*), **niña** (*girl*), and **mujer** (*woman*) are feminine, while **padre** (*father*), **niño** (*boy*), and **hombre** (*man*) are masculine. But why is **cine** masculine and **lámpara** feminine? There really is no logical reason. So, the only way to learn Spanish vocabulary is with the Spanish word for "the." You don't memorize **fruta** but **la fruta**, not **piano** but **el piano**.

Here's a helpful hint: most nouns that end in **-o** are masculine (**el piano, el libro, el disco**), and those ending in **-a** are almost always feminine (**la sopa, la gasolina, la fiesta**). With nouns ending in other letters, just memorize the article (the word for "the") along with the word: **el cine, la clase**, and so on.

Now that you have learned some Spanish words and grammar, let's see if you can figure out the meaning of these ten sentences. Repeat them aloud after your teacher:

**1. El hotel es moderno.**

**2. El doctor es importante.**

**3. El presidente es popular.**

**6. El dragón es horrible.**

**4. El actor es famoso.**

**7. El auto es americano.**

**5. La fruta es tropical.**

**8. El chocolate es delicioso.**

**9. La televisión es interesante.**

**10. La escuela es necesaria.**

 ## Actividad A

Match the following words with the correct pictures:

| | |
|---|---|
| el barbero | el gato |
| la bicicleta | el hotel |
| el camello | el insecto |
| el dragón | el periódico |
| la escuela | la rosa |

1. _____

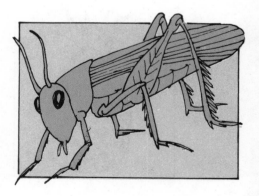

2. _____

3. _____

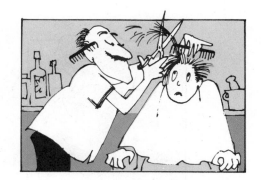

6. _____

4. _____

7. _____

5. _____

8. _____

9. _____

10. _____

 ## Actividad B

Label the following pictures. Make sure to use **el** or **la**:

1. _____

3. _____

2. _____

4. _____

5. _____

8. _____

6. _____

9. _____

7. _____

10. _____

11. _____

14. _____

12. _____

15. _____

13. _____

16. _____

17. _____    18. _____

## Actividad C

Write the Spanish word for "the" before each noun: **el** if the noun is masculine, **la** if the noun is feminine:

1. _*la*_ fiesta

2. _*el*_ tren

3. _*la*_ gasolina

4. _*el*_ animal

5. _*el*_ mosquito

6. _*el*_ restaurante

7. _*el*_ hombre

8. _*la*_ niña

9. _*la*_ profesora

10. _*el*_ disco

11. _*la*_ madre

12. _*el*_ niño

13. _*el*_ profesor

14. _*la*_ clase

15. _*el*_ padre

16. _*el*_ aeropuerto

## Actividad D

Complete each sentence correctly by writing one or more of the adjectives listed at the right:

Example: El hotel es ___grande, popular, famoso___.

1. El presidente es _____.          terrible

2. La flor es _____.          tropical

3. El tigre es _____.          natural

4. El café es _____.          grande

5. El auto es _____.          importante

6. El actor es _____.          delicioso

7. El color es _____.          popular

8. El tren es _____.          famoso

9. El parque es _____.          rápido

10. El hombre es _____.          americano

## Actividad E

**Sí o no.** If the statement is true, write **Sí.** If it is false, write **No.** (Watch out—there are differences of opinion!):

1. El mosquito es popular.          _____

2. La televisión es interesante.          _____

3. La profesora es inteligente.          _____

4. El doctor es necesario.          _____

5. El automóvil es rápido.          _____

## Actividad F

In each blank, write a noun that completes the sentence:

1. La _____ es grande.

2. El _____ es romántico.

3. La _____ es importante.

4. El _____ es rápido.

5. La _____ es inteligente.

6. El _____ es necesario.

7. La _____ es famosa.

8. El _____ es moderno.

9. El _____ es delicioso.

# Información personal

You now know enough Spanish to tell the class a little about yourself. Here's a list of words. Pick out all the words that you would use to describe yourself and include them in the sentence **Yo soy** . . . (*I am* . . . ). Be careful! Your classmates will show whether they agree with you or not by saying **Sí** or **No:**

| | |
|---|---|
| **estudiante** | **inteligente** |
| **grande** | **interesante** |
| **horrible** | **natural** |
| **importante** | **popular** |
| **imposible** | **terrible** |

**Yo soy** _____

_____

# 2 La familia

## How to Make Things Plural

### 1 Vocabulario

**la madre**

**el padre**

**el abuelo**

**la abuela**

**el hijo / el hermano**

**la hija / la hermana**

**el perro**

**el gato**

**2** Here we have one big happy family. It's obvious who all the members are. Let's take a closer look:

La familia Rodríguez es grande. Carlos y María son los hijos de la familia Rodríguez. Alberto y Rosa son los abuelos. El padre de la familia se llama Antonio. La madre se llama Carmen. Carlos y María son hermanos. Es una familia de seis personas. Amigo y Patitas son dos animales. Amigo es el perro y Patitas es el gato. La familia es de México. ¿Cómo se llaman los miembros de tu familia?

**es** *is*  **grande** *large*
 **y** *and*   **son** *are*   **de** *of*

**se llama** *is called, is named*

**seis** *six*

**¿Cómo se llaman . . . ?** *What are the names of . . . ?*  **tu** *your*

## Actividad A
Match the words with the pictures:

| | | |
|---|---|---|
| **la abuela** | **el gato** | **el padre** |
| **el abuelo** | **el hermano** | **los padres** |
| **los abuelos** | **la madre** | **el perro** |
| **la hermana** | | |

1. _____

3. _____

2. _____

4. _____

**5.** _____

**8.** _____

**6.** _____

**9.** _____

**7.** _____

**10.** _____

## Actividad B

Match the names with the people or pets:

1. Rosa _____ el abuelo

2. Carlos _____ el gato

3. María _____ la hija

4. Antonio _____ el padre

5. Patitas _____ el perro

6. Alberto _____ la abuela

7. Carmen _____ el hermano

8. Amigo _____ la madre

## Actividad C

**Sí o no.** Tell whether each statement is true or false. If your answer is **No,** give the correct answer:

1. El perro y el gato son **animales.** _____

2. Carlos y **Rosa** son los hijos. _____

3. Carlos y María son **hermanos.** _____

4. Antonio es el **hijo** de Alberto. _____

5. Amigo es el **padre** de la familia. _____

6. Alberto y Rosa son **los abuelos.** _____

7. El gato se llama **Patitas.** _____

8. El padre de mi madre es mi **abuela.** _____

**3**    Here's something new. All of the nouns you learned in Lesson 1 were SINGULAR (one). Now you have also seen nouns that are PLURAL (more than one). How do we change words from the singular to the plural in Spanish? Look carefully:

| I | II |
|---|---|
| el hijo | los hijos |
| el hermano | los hermanos |
| el padre | los padres |
| el abuelo | los abuelos |
| el gato | los gatos |
| la hija | las hijas |
| la hermana | las hermanas |
| la madre | las madres |
| la abuela | las abuelas |

Let's start by comparing the two groups. Underline the nouns in Groups I and II. Now look at them carefully and fill in the rest of the rule.

In Spanish, if a noun ends in a vowel (**a, e, i, o, u**), add the

letter _____ to the singular form of the noun to make it plural.

**4**    Now look carefully at these two groups:

| I | II |
|---|---|
| el animal | los animales |
| el doctor | los doctores |
| el tren | los trenes |
| la mujer | las mujeres |

Do the nouns in Group I end in a vowel? _____ How do they

end? _____ What letters do you add to make them

plural? _____ Here's the rule:

In Spanish, if a noun ends in a consonant (for example, **l, n, r**),

add the letters _____ to the singular form of the noun to make it plural.

**5**

Now underline all the words in Group I that mean "the." Look carefully at Group II, do the same, and fill in the rest of the rule:

The plural form of **el** is _____ .

The plural form of **la** is _____ .

**los** and **las** mean _____ .

REMEMBER: There are four words for "the" in Spanish: **el, la, los, las.**

## Actividad D

Fill in the correct Spanish word for "the". Use **el, la, los,** or **las.** Look back to Lesson 1 if necessary:

1. _____ gatos

2. _____ hermano

3. _____ perros

4. _____ niñas

5. _____ familia

6. _____ autos

7. _____ padres

8. _____ insecto

9. _____ mujer

10. _____ fiesta

11. _____ hija

12. _____ frutas

13. _____ lámpara

14. _____ discos

15. _____ bicicletas

16. _____ flor

17. _____ animal    19. _____ cines

18. _____ hombre    20. _____ amigo

## Actividad E
Make the following words plural. Use the correct Spanish for "the":

1. el padre     _____

2. el color     _____

3. el tren      _____

4. la blusa     _____

5. el auto      _____

6. la ambulancia  _____

7. el tigre     _____

8. el hombre    _____

9. el niño      _____

10. el profesor  _____

11. la hija     _____

12. el animal    _____

13. la clase    _____

14. la rosa     _____

15. el abuelo    _____

16. el plato    _____

**17.** la bicicleta   _____

**18.** la mujer   _____

**19.** la flor   _____

**20.** el cine   _____

 **Actividad F**
Identify:

**1.** _____

2. _____

6. _____

3. _____

7. _____

4. _____

8. _____

5. _____

9. _____

# Conversación

## Vocabulario

**Buenos días.** *Good morning. Hello.*
**¿Cómo te llamas?** *What's your name?*
**me llamo** *my name is*
**¿Cómo estás?** *How are you?*
**bien** *well*
**gracias** *thanks, thank you*

**tú** *you*
**regular** *OK, so-so*
**Hasta la vista.** *Good-bye*
**Adiós.** *Good-bye*
**Hasta mañana.** *See you tomorrow.*

# Información personal

Complete the picture with the other members of your family and then provide their names:

Me llamo: _____

Madre: _____

Padre: _____

Hermano(s): _____

Hermana(s): _____

Abuelo(s): _____

Abuela(s): _____

Perro(s): _____

Gato(s): _____

# Diálogo

Create your own dialog by filling in the missing words, chosen from the following list:

| | | | |
|---|---|---|---|
| adiós | cómo | llama | me |
| bien | días | llamas | regular |
| buenos | la vista | mañana | tú |

# 3 La clase y la escuela

## The Indefinite Articles

**1  Vocabulario**

Read the following words aloud after your teacher:

**el profesor**

**la profesora**

**la escuela**

**el alumno**

**la alumna**

**el papel**

**el libro**

**el lápiz**

**la pluma**

**la ventana**

**la pizarra**

**la puerta**

**la mesa**

# Actividad A
Identify:

1. _____

4. _____

2. _____

5. _____

3. _____

6. _____

7. _____

10. _____

8. _____

11. _____

9. _____

12. _____

## Actividad B

Fill in the correct definite article **el, la, los,** or **las:**

1. _____ libros
2. _____ escuela
3. _____ lápiz
4. _____ mesa
5. _____ papeles

6. _____ ventanas
7. _____ alumnos
8. _____ pluma
9. _____ profesor
10. _____ alumna

**2** Now that you know the new words, read the following story and see if you can understand it:

La clase de español es interesante. La profesora de la clase se llama Carmen López. La señorita López es una persona inteligente. En la clase ella usa una

**ella** *she*

pluma, un lápiz y muchos libros. En la lección, usa una pizarra.

Hay muchos alumnos en la clase. Pedro y Juana son alumnos de la clase de español. El muchacho y la muchacha son populares. La madre de Pedro es profesora. El padre de Juana es doctor.

**hay** *there is, there are*
**muchos** *many*

La clase es grande. Hay dos puertas y muchas ventanas.

**dos** *two*

## Actividad C

**Sí o no.** Read the story again. If the statement is true, write **Sí**. If it is false, write **No** and correct the wrong information:

1. La clase de español **no** es interesante. _____

2. La profesora de la clase se llama **Lola** López. _____

3. Pedro y Juana son **hermanos.** _____

4. **El abuelo** de Juana es doctor. _____

5. La profesora usa una **pizarra** en la lección. _____

## Actividad D

Fill in the blanks about the story:

1. La señorita López es _____ de la clase.

2. En la clase ella usa _____, _____

   y _____.

3. Hay _____ en la clase.

4. La madre de Pedro es _____.

5. El padre de Juana es _____.

**3** Look at the story again. There are two new little words that you read several times. Can you find these two new words? They are _____ and _____. If you answered **un** and **una,** you were right. These are the Spanish words for "a" or "an." Can you figure out when to use **un** and when to use **una?** Look carefully:

|  I  |  II  |
|-----|------|
| *el* libro | *un* libro |
| *el* lápiz | *un* lápiz |
| *el* muchacho | *un* muchacho |
| *el* doctor | *un* doctor |

**4** Let's start by comparing the two groups of nouns. Are the nouns in Group I masculine or feminine? _____?

How do you know? _____

What does **el** mean?_____ Now look at Group II. Which word has replaced **el?**_____ What does **un** mean?_____

**5** Now look at some more examples:

|  I  |  II  |
|-----|------|
| *la* clase | *una* clase |
| *la* persona | *una* persona |
| *la* pluma | *una* pluma |
| *la* profesora | *una* profesora |

Are the nouns in Group I masculine or feminine? _____

How do you know? _____ What does **la** mean?

_____ Now look at Group II. Which word has replaced **la?**

_____ What does **una** mean? _____

**6** Let's summarize:

**un** is used before a masculine noun to express "a" or "an."
**una** is used before a feminine noun to express "a" or "an."

**7** In the story on page 36, you may have noticed something about these sentences:

**La madre de Pedro es profesora.**
**El padre de Juana es doctor.**

That's right. We do not use **un** or **una** with a trade or profession:

**Ella es profesora.**   *She is a teacher.*

But look at this sentence:

**Ella es *una* profesora *mexicana*.** *She is a Mexican teacher.*

The indefinite article **un** or **una** IS used when the trade or profession is accompanied by an adjective.

 ## Actividad E

Let's try some more examples. Complete these sentences:

**1.** El señor López es _____ *(a doctor)*.

**2.** El señor López es _____ *(a Mexican doctor)*.

**3.** La señora Rodríguez es _____ *(a teacher)*.

**4.** La señora Rodríguez es _____ *(an interesting teacher)*.

**5.** Juanito es _____ *(a student)*.

**6.** Juanito es _____ *(an intelligent student).*

**7.** María es _____ *(an actress).*

**8.** María es _____ *(a popular actress).*

## Actividad F

Match the words with the pictures:

| | |
|---|---|
| **un alumno** | **una pizarra** |
| **un lápiz** | **una pluma** |
| **un libro** | **una profesora** |
| **una mesa** | **una puerta** |
| **un papel** | **una ventana** |

**1.** _____

**3.** _____

**2.** _____

**4.** _____

5. _____

8. _____

6. _____

9. _____

7. _____

10. _____

## Actividad G
Substitute **un** or **una** for **el** and **la**:

1. la lección   _____

2. el alumno   _____

3. la niña   _____

4. el profesor   _____

5. el parque   _____

6. la escuela   _____

7. el abuelo   _____

8. el hijo   _____

## Actividad H
Now try some on your own. Fill in **un** or **una**:

1. _____ alumna

2. _____ profesor

3. _____ papel

4. _____ libro

5. _____ lápiz

6. _____ pluma

7. _____ mesa

8. _____ pizarra

9. _____ ventana

10. _____ puerta

11. _____ lección

12. _____ señorita

13. _____ tren

14. _____ café

15. _____ bicicleta

16. _____ perro

# Conversación

## Vocabulario

¿**dónde?** *where?*
**está** *is*
**aquí** *here*
**mi** *my*
**muy** *very*

**están** *are*
**el diccionario** *the dictionary*
**tú estás** *you are*
**preparado** *prepared*

# Preguntas personales

Answer the questions in complete Spanish sentences:

1. ¿Dónde está el profesor / la profesora?

   _____

2. ¿Cómo se llama tu profesor / profesora?

   _____

3. ¿Dónde está tu pluma?

   _____

4. ¿Dónde están tus libros?

   _____

5. ¿Dónde están tus papeles?

   _____

# Información personal

The school year has just begun, and you are making a shopping list of school supplies that you will need. What would you include in your list? Write at least five items in Spanish:

1. _____

2. _____

3. _____

4. _____

5. _____

# Diálogo

Complete this dialog with the pupil's responses. Choose from the following list:

Aquí está mi libro, Señorita López.
Gracias. El español es mi clase favorita.
Buenos días, Señorita López.

Yo me llamo Federico.
Muy bien. ¿Y usted?
Aquí está mi lápiz.

# Los verbos

## How to Express Actions: **-AR** Verbs

**1**  The words that follow are all verbs. They express actions. See if you can guess their meanings:

**comprar** *to buy*

**entrar** *to enter*

**contestar**

*to answer*

**escuchar**

*to listen; to heed*

**45**

**estudiar** *to study*

**hablar** *to speak*

**mirar** *to look*

**pasar** *to pass; to cross*

**preguntar** *to ask*

**trabajar** *to work*

**usar** *to use;* *to wear*        **visitar** *to visit*

**2** You have just learned 12 important "action words," or verbs. Notice that they all end in **-ar**: **entr*ar*** (*to enter*), **trabaj*ar*** (*to work*), and so on.

If we want to use these words in a sentence, we must first make some changes. First, let's learn some subjects:

**yo** (*I*)

**tú** (*you*)

**él** (*he*)

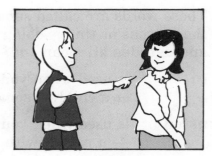

**ella** (*she*)

**usted** (*you*)

**ustedes** (*you*)

**nosotros** (*we* [boys; boys and girls])

**nosotras** (*we* [girls])

**ellos** (*they* [boys; boys and girls])

**ellas** (*they* [girls])

These words are called subject pronouns. Subject pronouns refer to the persons or things doing the action. Did you notice that **tú, usted,** and **ustedes** all mean *you*?

**tú**      is used when you are speaking to a close relative, a friend, or a child — someone with whom you are familiar.

**usted**    is used when you are speaking to a stranger or a grown-up — a person with whom you are or should be formal.

**ustedes**  is used when you are speaking to two or more persons, whether familiarly or formally.

## Actividad A

Write the subject pronoun you would use if you were speaking to the following people. Would you use **tú, usted,** or **ustedes**?

1. el profesor _____

2. la niña _____

3. la señora Ruiz _____

4. Pedro y Carlos _____

5. María _____

6. las mujeres _____

7. Roberto _____

8. los abuelos _____

**3**

Now that you know subject pronouns, you are ready to learn the verb forms. Simply remove the **-ar** from the end of the verb and substitute another ending that goes with the subject you want. Here are the endings that go with the different subjects:

| SUBJECT | ENDING |
|---------|--------|
| **yo** | **-o** |
| **tú** | **-as** |
| **usted** | **-a** |
| **él**<br>**ella** | **-a** |
| **nosotros**<br>**nosotras** | **-amos** |
| **ustedes** | **-an** |
| **ellos**<br>**ellas** | **-an** |

Let's see how it works. Take, for example, the verb **hablar** (*to speak*). If you want to say *I speak*, take **yo**, then remove the **-ar** from **hablar**, and add the ending **-o**:

**hablar**

**yo hablo**     *I speak, I am speaking*

We do the same for all the other subjects, and we get:

| | |
|---|---|
| **tú hablas** | *you speak, you are speaking* (familiar singular) |
| **usted habla** | *you speak, you are speaking* (formal singular) |
| **él habla** | *he speaks, he is speaking* |
| **ella habla** | *she speaks, she is speaking* |
| **nosotros hablamos** <br> **nosotras hablamos** } | *we speak, we are speaking* |
| **ustedes hablan** | *you speak, you are speaking* (plural) |
| **ellos hablan** <br> **ellas hablan** } | *they speak, they are speaking* |

Note that there are two possible meanings for each verb form: **yo hablo** may mean *I speak* or *I am speaking*; **tú hablas** may mean *you speak* or *you are speaking*; and so on.

Now can you do one? Take the verb **comprar** (*to buy*). Remove the **-ar,** look at the subjects and add the correct endings:

yo compr_____ *I buy, I am buying*

tú compr_____ *you buy, you are buying* (talking to a friend)

usted compr_____ *you buy, you are buying* (talking to a stranger)

él compr_____ *he buys, he is buying*

ella compr_____ *she buys, she is buying*

nosotros compr_____ *we buy, we are buying*

ustedes compr_____ *you buy, you are buying* (talking to more than one person)

ellos/ellas compr_____ *they buy, they are buying*

**4**

Fine! But there's a hitch. The subjects we used so far are all pronouns (**yo, tú, usted, él, ella, nosotros, ustedes, ellos, ellas**). What if the subject is not a pronoun but a name or a person or a thing? For example: **Pedro, la niña, los abuelos, el perro.** The answer is simple. **Pedro** = *he,* **la niña** = *she,* **los abuelos** = *they,* and **el perro** = *he* (there is no separate word for *it* in Spanish).

Therefore, the ending on the verb that goes with **Pedro** is **-a**:

**Pedro compra**

Other examples:

**la muchacha compra**
**los padres compran**
**el perro entra**
**María y yo entramos**

In the fourth example, above, do you see why the **-amos** ending is used? Since **María y yo** = **nosotros,** the appropriate ending is the one that goes with **nosotros** or **nosotras.**

**5**

An important point regarding the use of subject pronouns (**yo, tú,** etc.): In Spanish, the pronoun is often omitted if the meaning is clear. For example, *I speak Spanish* may be either **yo hablo español** or simply **hablo español.** The **yo** isn't really necessary except for emphasis, since the **-o** ending in **hablo** occurs only with the **yo** form. Another example: *we are working* may be **nosotros trabajamos** or simply **trabajamos,** since the verb form that ends in **-amos** cannot be used with any other subject pronoun.

In fact, any subject pronoun may be omitted if it's not needed for clarity or emphasis:

| | |
|---|---|
| —¿**Dónde está María?** | *Where is Maria?* |
| —**Está en el mercado.** | *She is in the market.* |
| —¿**Qué hace?** | *What is she doing?* |
| —**Compra bananas.** | *She is buying bananas.* |

In the lessons that follow, we will sometimes omit the subject pronoun.

## Actividad B

Here are eight Spanish "action words." Tell who is "doing the action" by writing every pronoun that can be used with the verb. Then write what each verb means:

Example: __ustéd, él, ella__ habla _you speak, he speaks, she speaks_

1. _____ contesto _____

2. _____ compras _____

3. _____ entro _____

4. _____ estudian _____

5. _____ trabaja _____

6. _____ usan _____

7. _____ pregunto _____

8. _____ visitas _____

## Actividad C

Write the form of the verb that is used with each subject. Remember to remove the **-ar** of the infinitive before adding the correct ending:

Example: hablar: yo _____ **hablo** _____

1. usar: yo _____

2. trabajar: tú _____

3. contestar: él _____

4. preguntar: ella _____

**5.** escuchar: usted _____

**6.** visitar: nosotras _____

**7.** pasar: ellos _____

**8.** entrar: Alberto y yo _____


## Actividad D

Now complete the Spanish sentences by adding the correct verb form:

**1.** (speak)    Yo _____ español.

**2.** (work)    Tú _____ mucho.

**3.** (buy)    Nosotros _____ muchas cosas.

**4.** (enter)    Ellas _____ en la clase.

**5.** (study)    Los alumnos _____ en la escuela.

**6.** (pass)    El perro _____ por el parque.

**7.** (visit)    Yo _____ a la profesora.

**8.** (listen)    Tú _____ en la clase.

**9.** (answer)    Pedro y yo _____.

**10.** (use)    Ricardo _____ el diccionario.

**6** Here is a story using some of the verbs you have just learned. See if you understand it and can spot the verbs:

La señorita Pacheco es profesora y trabaja en una escuela grande. Los alumnos estudian español, inglés, matemáticas y otras cosas. La profesora usa muchos libros y papeles en la lección. Cuando ella habla, yo escucho con atención. Cuando la profesora pregunta, yo contesto bien.

**otra(s)** *other*
**la cosa** *the thing*
**cuando** *when*

 ## Actividad E

**Sí o no.** The following statements are based on the story you have just read. If the statement is true, write **Sí.** If it is false, write **No** and correct the wrong information:

**1.** La señorita Pacheco trabaja en **casa.** _____

2. Los alumnos estudian **francés.** _____

3. La profesora usa **una bicicleta.** _____

4. **Los alumnos** escuchan bien. _____

5. **La profesora** pregunta y **los alumnos** contestan. _____

6. La señorita Pacheco es una **alumna** muy buena. _____

7. **Los padres** estudian mucho. _____

8. Cuando la profesora **escucha,** los alumnos **hablan.** _____

9. **La profesora estudia** inglés y matemáticas. _____

 ## Actividad F

Match the descriptions with the correct pictures:

Nosotros entramos.    Ellos hablan español.
Los estudiantes contestan.    Usted compra una rosa.
Los hombres trabajan.    Yo escucho.
El profesor pregunta.    Los animales pasan.

1. _____     2. _____

**3.** _____

**6.** _____

**4.** _____

**7.** _____

**5.** _____

**8.** _____

# Conversación

## Vocabulario

**desear** *to wish;* **yo deseo** *I'd like to*
**¿Vamos a entrar?** *Are we going in?*
**buena** *good*
**rubio** *blond*

**guapo** *handsome*
**moreno** *dark*
**¡Vamos!** *Let's go!*
**¡Buena suerte!** *Good luck!*

# Diálogo

Fill in the words that are missing in the dialog. Choose from the following list:

vamos      discoteca      magnífica
guapo      suerte      hablar
bailar      mesa

# Información personal

List some of the things you do every day by supplying verbs to complete the following sentences. (Some sentences can be completed with more than one verb.):

Yo _____ por teléfono.

_____ en la casa.

_____ la televisión.

_____ la radio.

_____ la lección.

_____ el libro.

_____ en la clase.

# Repaso I
# (Lecciones 1–4)

Nouns in Spanish are either masculine or feminine. The definite article (English *the*) before masculine nouns is **el** and before feminine nouns **la**:

|  |  |
|---|---|
| *el* muchacho | *la* muchacha |
| *el* profesor | *la* profesora |

**a.** To make Spanish nouns ending in a vowel (**a, e, i, o, u**) plural, add **s** to the singular form. The definite article (*the*) before masculine plural nouns is **los** and before feminine plural nouns **las**:

|  |  |
|---|---|
| *el* perro | *los* perros |
| *la* alumna | *las* alumnas |

**b.** If a Spanish noun ends in a consonant, add **es** to form the plural:

|  |  |
|---|---|
| el profesor | los profesores |
| la flor | las flores |

There are two ways to say "a" or "an" in Spanish:

**un**  is used before a masculine singular noun:

*un* **alumno**
*un* **lápiz**

**una** is used before a feminine singular noun:

*una* **alumna**
*una* **mesa**

**a.** The subject pronouns are:

| | |
|---|---|
| **yo** *(I)* | **nosotros, nosotras** *(we)* |
| **tú** *(you)* | |
| **usted** *(you)* | **ustedes** *(you)* |
| **él** *(he, it)* | **ellos** *(they)* |
| **ella** *(she, it)* | **ellas** *(they)* |

**b.** In order to have a correct verb with each subject, the original form of the verb is changed so that it agrees with the subject pronoun or noun. Drop the ending **-ar** and add the endings that belong to the different subjects. This step is called CONJUGATION.

Example: **usar**

| If the subject is | | add | | to the remaining stem: | |
|---|---|---|---|---|---|
| | **yo** | add | **o** | | **yo** us**o** |
| | **tú** | | **as** | | **tú** us**as** |
| | **usted** | | **a** | | **usted** us**a** |
| | **él** | | **a** | | **él** us**a** |
| | **ella** | | **a** | | **ella** us**a** |
| | **nosotros**<br>**nosotras** | | **amos** | | **nosotros**<br>**nosotras** } us**amos** |
| | **ustedes** | | **an** | | **ustedes** us**an** |
| | **ellos**<br>**ellas** | | **an** | | **ellos**<br>**ellas** } us**an** |

We have just conjugated the verb **usar** in the present tense.

## Actividad A

Identify the pictures in Spanish and then circle the Spanish words in the puzzle on page 65. The words may be read from left to right, right to left, up or down, or diagonally:

1. _____

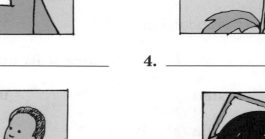

4. _____

2. _____

5. _____

3. _____

6. _____

7. _____

10. _____

8. _____

11. _____

9. _____

12. _____

**13.** _____

**16.** _____

**14.** _____

**17.** _____

**15.** _____

**18.** _____

```
M A B U E L O S O E
A M A B F L O R D T
D I S C O Á T N E N
R G G T A P L U M A
E A A A L I B R O I
I G J E U Z V X R D
L I P S M E S A R U
H A M N N O P Ñ E T
P O L L O Q R I P S
S E R B M O H N T E
```

## Actividad B

Find the hidden classroom objects. There are ten classroom objects hidden in the picture. Circle them in the picture and list them below in Spanish:

1. _____

2. _____

3. _____

4. _____

5. _____

6. _____

7. _____

8. _____

9. _____

10. _____

## Actividad C

Here are ten pictures of people doing things. Describe each picture, using the correct form of one of the following verbs:

| | |
|---|---|
| comprar | mirar |
| contestar | pasar |
| entrar | preguntar |
| escuchar | trabajar |
| estudiar | usar |
| hablar | visitar |

**1.** El alumno _____ el calendario.

**3.** Las señoritas _____.

**2.** Nosotros _____ a la amiga.

**4.** Yo _____ el diccionario.

**5.** La mujer _____.

**8.** Ellos _____ el auto.

**6.** Los alumnos _____.

**9.** Los hombres _____.

**7.** El perro _____.

**10.** La muchacha _____ bien.

# Actividad D

How many of the words describing the pictures in the puzzle below do you remember? Fill in the Spanish words, then read down the boxed column of letters to find the word that completes this sentence:

El español es _____.

1.

2.

3.

4.

5.

6.

7.

8.

## Actividad E

Picture Story. Can you read this story? Much of it is in picture form. Whenever you come to a picture, read it as if it were a Spanish word:

Pepe es un  . Él estudia español en la  .

La  de Pepe se llama Isabel. El  se llama

Jorge. El padre es  . Él trabaja en un  .

La madre de Pepe es  . Ella trabaja en una

moderna. Pepe estudia en una  grande.

En la  usa muchas cosas: un  , una  ,

un  y  . En la  de Pepe hay dos

animales. Amigo es un 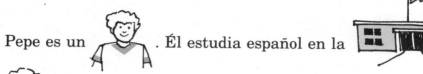 , y Patitas es un  .

# Segunda
## Parte

# 5 Los verbos continúan

## How to Ask Questions and Say "No" in Spanish

**1** Look at the following sentences:

**Pedro baila.**

**Ricardo no baila.**

**Yo practico la lección.**

**Yo no practico la lección.**

73

**Ellos cantan.**

**Ellos no cantan.**

Do you see what's happening here? If you want to make a sentence negative in Spanish, what word is placed directly in front of the verb?

_____ If you wrote **no,** you are correct.

No matter what we say in English (*doesn't, don't, aren't, won't,* and the like), in Spanish the rule is always the same: To make a sentence negative, put the word **no** in front of the verb.

Here are some examples:

**Ella *no* trabaja.**     { *She doesn't work.* <br> { *She isn't working.*

**Nosotros *no* entramos.**     { *We don't enter.* <br> { *We're not entering.*

**Usted *no* escucha.**     { *You don't listen.* <br> { *You're not listening.*

## Actividad A

Make the following sentences negative. Then write the meaning of each negative sentence on the line below it:

**1.** Yo hablo.     _____

_____

**2.** Ustedes usan papeles.     _____

_____

**3.** Tú contestas. _____

_____

**4.** Ellos escuchan. _____

_____

**5.** María baila. _____

_____

**6.** Los automóviles pasan. _____

_____

**7.** Ella practica. _____

_____

**8.** La profesora trabaja. _____

_____

**9.** El actor entra. _____

_____

**10.** Los padres preguntan. _____

_____

**2**

¡**Magnífico!** You now know how to make a Spanish sentence negative. But do you know how to ask a question in Spanish? It's just as simple. Look at the following sentences:

| | |
|---|---|
| **Usted habla español.** | *¿Habla usted español?* |
| **Ella canta.** | *¿Canta ella?* |
| **Los alumnos estudian.** | *¿Estudian los alumnos?* |
| **Pedro desea hablar.** | *¿Desea Pedro hablar?* |

What did we do? We put the subject (**usted, ella, los alumnos, Pedro** — or any other) after the verb when we ask a question. Observe that we do not use *do, does, am, are, is* in Spanish. You have probably also noticed that, in addition to the regular question mark at the end, an upside-down question mark is placed at the beginning of a Spanish question. That's all there is to it.

## Actividad B

Make questions of these sentences and tell what they mean:

1. Usted pregunta. _____

_____

2. Los muchachos contestan. _____

_____

3. El amigo entra. _____

_____

4. La madre canta. _____

_____

5. Los hombres compran. _____

_____

6. El hermano visita. _____

_____

7. Las hijas practican. _____

_____

8. El médico escucha. _____

_____

9. La mujer trabaja. _____

_____

10. Nosotras bailamos. _____

## Actividad C

Match the English meanings in the right column with the Spanish sentences in the left column. Write the matching letter in the space provided:

1. Usted no usa un lápiz. _____ **a.** They don't speak Spanish.

2. ¿Trabaja usted mucho? _____ **b.** Is there a book in the class?

3. ¿Estudian ustedes? _____ **c.** You don't use a pencil.

4. Ella no contesta en la clase. _____ **d.** Do you work hard (a lot)?

5. ¿Es inteligente el profesor? _____ **e.** The actor does not dance.

6. ¿Hay un libro en la clase? _____ **f.** My teacher doesn't talk a lot.

7. ¿Escuchas tú la música? _____ **g.** Are you studying?

8. ¿Pasan las chicas ahora? _____ **h.** She doesn't answer in class.

9. El actor no baila. _____ **i.** Are the girls passing now?

10. ¿Canta él? _____ **j.** Is the teacher intelligent?

11. Ellos no hablan español. _____ **k.** Are you listening to the music?

12. Mi profesor no habla mucho. _____ **l.** Does he sing?

**3**  Here's a short story. Can you understand it?

Muchas personas usan automóviles en América. Los hombres y las mujeres usan automóviles para ir al trabajo. Los profesores (y muchos estudiantes) usan automóviles para ir a la escuela. Los médicos necesitan automóviles para ir al hospital. ¿Necesitas un automóvil? Sí, señor. Necesito un automóvil para ir al supermercado. ¿Y qué necesita un automóvil? Un automóvil necesita gasolina, mucha gasolina. También, necesita un garaje.

**ir** *to go*
**al** *to the*

**también** *also*

## Actividad D
Answer the following questions in Spanish:

1. ¿Es importante el automóvil en América?

   _____

   _____

2. ¿Usan automóviles los médicos?

   _____

   _____

3. ¿Por qué necesita usted un automóvil?

   _____

   _____

4. ¿Qué necesita un automóvil?

   _____

   _____

5. ¿Qué más necesitas para un automóvil?

   _____

   _____

## Actividad E

Ask your teacher if he/she does the following. Remember to use **usted** forms when speaking to your teacher:

1. _____

2. _____

3. _____

## Actividad F

Ask your friend if he/she does the following. Remember to use **tú** forms when speaking to your friend:

**1.** _____

**2.** _____

**3.** _____

# Preguntas personales

Answer these questions about yourself:

1. ¿Bailas bien?

_____

2. ¿Cantas en la clase?

_____

3. ¿Hablas español?

_____

4. ¿Escuchas con atención?

_____

# Información personal

**¡Felicitaciones!**   Congratulations! You have been picked the student most likely to succeed. Tell your friends what you do in your spare time to make you so successful. Start each sentence with **Yo . . .** or **Yo no . . .**

Example: Yo no miro mucha televisión.

1. _____

2. _____

3. _____

4. _____

5. _____

# Conversación

## Vocabulario

**Buenas tardes.** *Good afternoon.*
**usado** *used*
**nuevo** *new*
**si** *if*

**claro** *of course*
**tiene** *you have*
**poco** *(a) little*
**el dinero** *the money*

# Diálogo

Fill in what the second person in the dialog would say. Choose from the following list:

    ¡Perfecto!

    Un automóvil pequeño. Es para ir al supermercado.

    Buenas tardes. Necesito un automóvil.

    Usado, si es bueno.

# 6 Uno, dos, tres . . .

## How to Count in Spanish; Numbers 1–30

**1** Repeat the numbers aloud after your teacher:

0 cero

| 1 uno | 11 once | 21 veinte y uno |
| 2 dos | 12 doce | 22 veinte y dos |
| 3 tres | 13 trece | 23 veinte y tres |
| 4 cuatro | 14 catorce | 24 veinte y cuatro |
| 5 cinco | 15 quince | 25 veinte y cinco |
| 6 seis | 16 diez y seis | 26 veinte y seis |
| 7 siete | 17 diez y siete | 27 veinte y siete |
| 8 ocho | 18 diez y ocho | 28 veinte y ocho |
| 9 nueve | 19 diez y nueve | 29 veinte y nueve |
| 10 diez | 20 veinte | 30 treinta |

## Actividad A

Match the Spanish number with the numeral and write it in the space provided:

1. cuatro _____ 5

2. dos _____ 20

3. trece _____ 9

4. veinte _____ 15

5. diez y ocho _____ 4

6. quince _____ 2

7. cinco _____ 13

8. nueve _____ 18

## Actividad B

Find the hidden numbers and write them out in Spanish:

_____  _____

_____  _____

_____  _____

_____  _____

**2** Here's a little poem about **"Diez gatitos"** *(Ten little kittens)*. Try singing it to the tune of "Ten little Indians":

> **Uno, dos, tres gatitos,**
> **cuatro, cinco, seis gatitos,**
> **siete, ocho, nueve gatitos,**
> **diez gatitos son.**
>
> **10, 9, 8 gatitos,**
> **7, 6, 5 gatitos,**
> **4, 3, 2 gatitos,**
> **un gatito es.**

## Actividad C

**La telefonista.** The telephone operator would like you to repeat some numbers in Spanish. You reply:

> Señorita, el número . . .

**1.** 456-3278 _____ cuatro-cinco-seis-tres-dos-siete-ocho _____

**2.** 879-4621 _____

**3.** 737-3456 _____

**4.** 455-6743 _____

**5.** 620-2987 _____

**6.** 080-2539 _____

**3**

In this story, Luis and his sister Graciela make a small profit. Read on to find out how they do it. But first learn your numbers, because there are lots of them in the story:

PERSONAS:  Luis, un niño de siete años.
Graciela, una niña de seis años.
El vendedor de billetes de lotería.
Un hombre.

**el vendedor** *the seller*
**el billete** *the ticket*
**la lotería** *the lottery*

VENDEDOR:  ¡El último billete! ¡El último billete!

**último** *last*

LUIS:  Deseamos el billete.

VENDEDOR:  Muy bien. Cuesta veinte centavos.

**muy bien** *very well*

LUIS:  ¡Está bien! Veinte centavos. (Cuenta.) Ocho, nueve, diez, once, doce, trece, catorce, quince, diez y seis, diez y siete. Tengo diez y siete centavos, señor. ¿Acepta usted los diez y siete centavos?

**cuesta** *it costs*
**el centavo** *cent, penny*
**¡Está bien!** *all right, O.K.*
**cuenta** *he counts*
**(yo) tengo** *I have*

**aceptar** *to accept*

| | |
|---|---|
| VENDEDOR: | No, señor. Son veinte centavos. |
| GRACIELA: | Yo tengo aquí tres centavos. |
| LUIS: | ¡Muy bien! Diez y siete y tres son veinte. |
| VENDEDOR: | ¡Exacto! Muchas gracias, niños. |
| UN HOMBRE: | Yo deseo un billete también. |
| VENDEDOR: | Imposible. Es el último billete. |
| HOMBRE: | Niños, ¿aceptan ustedes un dólar por el billete? |
| LUIS Y GRACIELA: | ¡Un dólar! Somos ricos. |

**somos** *we are*
**rico(s)** *rich*

## Actividad D

Complete these sentences, which are based on the conversation you
have just read:

**1.** Luis es un niño de _____ años.

**2.** Graciela es una niña de _____ años.

**3.** Ellos desean comprar _____.

**4.** El precio del billete es _____ centavos.

**5.** Luis cuenta _____ centavos.

**6.** Luis y Graciela compran el _____ billete.

## Actividad E

Your teacher will read some numbers to you. Write the numeral for the number you hear:

Example: you hear: **veinte.**     You write: **20**

1. _____     6. _____

2. _____     7. _____

3. _____     8. _____

4. _____     9. _____

5. _____     10. _____

## Actividad F

You will hear a number in English. Write out the number in Spanish:

1. _____     6. _____

2. _____     7. _____

3. _____     8. _____

4. _____     9. _____

5. _____     10. _____

**4** Now that you know the Spanish words for the numbers 1 to 30, let's try some arithmetic in Spanish. First you must learn the following expressions:

| | | | |
|---|---|---|---|
| **y** | *and, plus* ($+$) | **dividido por** | *divided by* ($\div$) |
| **menos** | *minus, less* ($-$) | **es** | *is, equals* ($=$) |
| **por** | *times* ($\times$) | **son** | *are, equals* ($=$) |

Examples: 
$2 + 2 = 4$ **dos y dos son cuatro**
$5 - 4 = 1$ **cinco menos cuatro es uno**
$3 \times 3 = 9$ **tres por tres son nueve**
$12 \div 2 = 6$ **doce dividido por dos son seis**

## Actividad G

Read the following numbers in Spanish. Then write out each problem in numerals:

1. Cinco y cinco son diez. _____

2. Veinte menos cinco son quince. _____

3. Nueve por dos son diez y ocho. _____

4. Seis y tres son nueve. _____

5. Cuatro dividido por dos son dos. _____

6. Diez y siete menos diez y seis es uno. _____

7. Once por uno son once. _____

8. Veinte dividido por cinco son cuatro. _____

9. Diez y ocho dividido por dos son nueve. _____

10. Diez y seis y tres son diez y nueve. _____

## Actividad H

Read the following examples in Spanish, then write them out in Spanish:

1. $2 + 3 = 5$ _____

2. $9 - 2 = 7$ _____

3. $4 \times 4 = 16$ _____

4. $8 \div 2 = 4$ _____

5. $22 + 3 = 25$ _____

**6.** $10 - 5 = 5$ _____

**7.** $24 + 5 = 29$ _____

**8.** $6 \div 3 = 2$ _____

**9.** $10 + 11 = 21$ _____

**10.** $18 - 7 = 11$ _____

## Actividad I

Circle the letter of the correct answer and then read the entire problem aloud:

**1.** Cuatro menos dos son
    (a) 2      (b) 4      (c) 6      (d) 8

**2.** Ocho y tres son
    (a) 12     (b) 11     (c) 10     (d) 9

**3.** Seis dividido por tres son
    (a) 1      (b) 3      (c) 2      (d) 4

**4.** Cuatro y cuatro son
    (a) 8      (b) 20     (c) 0      (d) 16

**5.** Ocho y siete son
    (a) 15     (b) 1      (c) 16     (d) 3

**6.** Dos menos uno es
    (a) 3      (b) 1      (c) 2      (d) 4

**7.** Tres por tres son
    (a) 6      (b) 8      (c) 9      (d) 2

**8.** Cuatro dividido por cuatro es
    (a) 1      (b) 8      (c) 0      (d) 10

**9.** Tres y cuatro y cinco son
    (a) 17     (b) 12     (c) 2      (d) 4

**10.** Veinte menos diez y ocho son
    (a) 10     (b) 9      (c) 2      (d) 8

# Actividad J

Add the columns in stages from top to bottom:

Example:

Ocho y seis son catorce.

Catorce y dos son diez y seis.

Diez y seis y cuatro son veinte.

Check your answers by adding from bottom to top:

1. _____

_____

_____

**2.** _____

_____

_____

**3.** _____

_____

_____

**4.** _____

_____

_____

# Conversation

## Vocabulario

**¿cuántos?** *how much?*
**claro que no** *of course not, no way*
**¿Qué te pasa?** *What's the matter with you?*
**hoy** *today*

**generalmente** *generally*
**eres** *you are*
**hacer cálculos** *to calculate, do math*
**este vendaje** *this bandage*

# Diálogo

You are asking all the questions today. Complete the dialog, choosing from the following list:

¿Cuántos son veinte dividido por dos?

¿Qué te pasa hoy?

¿Cuántos son tres y cuatro?

¿Cuántos son quince menos cinco?

# ▪ Información personal

Your school requires that every student fill out an I.D. card. Supply the following information in Spanish, writing out all the numbers:

1. Edad (*age*): _____ años

2. Número de hermanos: _____

3. Número de hermanas: _____

4. Número de miembros de la familia: _____

5. Número de animales domésticos: _____

6. Número de la casa: _____

7. Número de teléfono: _____

# 7 Otros verbos

## More Action Words: **-ER Verbs**

**1** The verbs that follow belong to the **-ER** family. See if you can guess their meanings:

**aprender**

**beber**

**comer**

**comprender**

**leer**

**responder**

**vender**

**ver**

**2** Here are eight more action words. You have probably noticed that

these verbs don't end in **-ar** but in _____. You'll recall how we made changes in **-ar** verbs by dropping the **-ar** and adding certain endings. Well, we must do the same thing with **-er** verbs, but the endings will be slightly different. Let's see what happens. A good example is the verb **vender** (*to sell*). If you want to say *I sell*, remove the **-er** ending of the infinitive and add **-o**, which is the ending for the **yo** form. Here are the forms for all the subjects:

|  |  |
|---|---|
| yo vend**o** | *I sell, I am selling* |
| tú vend**es** | *you sell, you are selling* (familiar singular) |
| usted vend**e** | *you sell, you are selling* (formal singular) |
| él vend**e** | *he sells, he is selling* |
| ella vend**e** | *she sells, she is selling* |
| nosotros }<br>nosotras } vend**emos** | *we sell, we are selling* |
| ustedes vend**en** | *you sell, you are selling* (plural) |
| ellos }<br>ellas } vend**en** | *they sell, they are selling* |

## Actividad A

Now let's practice with other **-er** verbs:

|  | aprender | comprender | leer | ver |
|---|---|---|---|---|
| yo | _____ | _____ | _____ | _____ |
| tú | _____ | _____ | _____ | _____ |
| usted | _____ | _____ | _____ | _____ |
| él | _____ | _____ | _____ | _____ |
| ella | _____ | _____ | _____ | _____ |
| nosotros | _____ | _____ | _____ | _____ |
| ustedes | _____ | _____ | _____ | _____ |
| ellos | _____ | _____ | _____ | _____ |
| ellas | _____ | _____ | _____ | _____ |

**3**

Now let's compare an **-ar** verb with and **-er** verb. How are they similar and how are they different?

<table>
<tr><td align="center">**trabajar**</td><td align="center">**comer**</td></tr>
<tr><td align="center">yo trabaj*o*</td><td align="center">yo com*o*</td></tr>
<tr><td align="center">tú trabaj*as*</td><td align="center">tú com*es*</td></tr>
<tr><td align="center">usted trabaj*a*</td><td align="center">usted com*e*</td></tr>
<tr><td align="center">él trabaj*a*</td><td align="center">él com*e*</td></tr>
<tr><td align="center">ella trabaj*a*</td><td align="center">ella com*e*</td></tr>
<tr><td align="center">nosotros trabaj*amos*</td><td align="center">nosotros com*emos*</td></tr>
<tr><td align="center">ustedes trabaj*an*</td><td align="center">ustedes com*en*</td></tr>
<tr><td align="center">ellos trabaj*an*</td><td align="center">ellos com*en*</td></tr>
<tr><td align="center">ellas trabaj*an*</td><td align="center">ellas com*en*</td></tr>
</table>

Notice that the **yo** form has the same ending in both **-ar** and **-er** verbs: **yo trabaj*o*, yo com*o*.** In all other forms, however, the **-ar** verbs have endings that are **a** or begin with **a,** while the **-er** verbs have endings that are **e** or begin with **e.**

**4**

Before we read the story in this lesson, there are two tiny points of grammar that should be covered: the contraction **al** and the personal **a.** In Spanish, the preposition **a** means *to:*

**Ellos caminan *a* la tienda.**   *They walk to the store.*
**Ellos corren *a* la escuela.**   *They run to the school.*

If the preposition **a** comes directly before the article **el** (*the*), the two words combine to form the word **al,** that is, **a + el = al:**

**Ella vende el libro *al* hombre.** *She sells the book to the man.*
**(*a* + *el* hombre = *al* hombre)**

There's another important use of the preposition **a.** It's called the personal **a.** Look at these sentences:

**Yo veo *a* Pedro.**              *I see Peter.*
**Yo contesto *a* la profesora.**  *I answer the teacher.*
**Yo amo *a* mi gato.**            *I love my cat.*

What is the extra word in the Spanish sentences that has no equivalent in the English sentences?_____

Did you notice that, when the direct object of a verb is a person or a pet (**Pedro, la profesora, mi gato**), the preposition **a** is placed before it even though the **a** has no equivalent in English?

Some more examples:

**Miro las casas.**      *I look at the houses.*
**Miro *a* los muchachos.**      *I look at the boys.*

**Visito la escuela.**      *I visit the school.*
**Visito *a* mi amigo.**      *I visit my friend.*

## Actividad B

Complete the following sentences. If the personal **a** is not needed, leave the blank empty. If **al** is needed, cross out **el:**

1. Comprendemos _____ la lección.

2. Comprendemos _____ el presidente.

3. Yo no veo _____ la muchacha.

4. Yo no veo _____ el billete.

5. Los alumnos escuchan _____ el disco.

6. Los alumnos escuchan _____ la señora Montano.

7. María visita _____ el director.

8. María visita _____ la clase.

9. No comprendo _____ la profesora.

10. No comprendo _____ la pregunta.

## 5 Now we are ready to read the story:

Lupita, una muchacha de once años, tiene un gato que se llama Patitas. Patitas es un gato bonito. Lupita siempre compra la comida para Patitas. Patitas no es grande pero come mucho. Patitas es muy inteligente y aprende rápidamente. El gato está muy contento cuando ve a Lupita. Patitas desea correr en el jardín. Cuando Lupita dice: «¡Patitas, Patitas!», el gato comprende y siempre responde: «¡Miau, miau!»

**tiene** *has*
**bonito** *pretty*
**siempre** *always*
  **la comida** *the food*
**rápidamente** *fast*

**correr** *to run*
  **el jardín** *the garden*

 ## Actividad C
Complete the sentences based on the story you have just read:

1. Lupita es una muchacha _____.

2. Patitas es _____ de Lupita.

3. Patitas necesita mucha _____.

4. El gato está contento cuando _____.

5. Cuando Lupita dice: «¡Patitas, Patitas!», el gato_____.

## Actividad D

Fill in the correct forms of the verbs. Be sure to drop all the **-ar** or **-er** endings before starting:

1. (visitar)    Nosotros _____ a la profesora.

2. (vender)    Pedro _____ billetes de lotería.

3. (practicar) Tú _____ la lección.

4. (leer)    Usted _____ el periódico.

5. (responder) Mi hermano _____ en español.

6. (usar)    Ellos _____ muchos libros.

7. (aprender) Ustedes _____ rápidamente.

8. (trabajar)  Mi padre _____ en una escuela moderna.

9. (ver)    Yo _____ a mi gato en el jardín.

10. (correr)   Ella _____ a la tienda con su perro.

## Actividad E

Change all of the sentences in Exercise D to the negative:

1. _____

2. _____

3. _____

4. _____

5. _____

6. _____

7. _____

8. _____

9. _____

10. _____

## Actividad F

Change all the sentences in Exercise D to questions:

1. _____

2. _____

3. _____

4. _____

5. _____

6. _____

7. _____

8. _____

9. _____

10. _____

## Actividad G

Match the sentences with the pictures they describe:

Nosotras leemos un libro.
El gato come.
El muchacho vende periódicos.
Yo respondo en la clase.
El hombre bebe el café.

Los alumnos aprenden mucho.
La muchacha no comprende.
El perro sabe bailar.
Vemos el avión.
Ellos corren al cine.

1. _____

3. _____

2. _____

4. _____

**5.** _____

**8.** _____

**6.** _____

**9.** _____

**7.** _____

**10.** _____

## Actividad H

Fill in a correct subject pronoun:

1. _____ vendo          6. _____ aprende

2. _____ bebes          7. _____ como

3. _____ leemos         8. _____ ven

4. _____ responden      9. _____ comprendemos

5. _____ ve            10. _____ vendes

# Información personal

Your school counselor wants to find out a few things about your personality. Finish each sentence in a way that tells us something about you.

Example: Leo ____el periódico____.

1. Aprendo _____.

2. Como _____.

3. Corro _____.

4. Respondo _____.

5. Trabajo _____.

6. Escucho _____.

# Conversación

## Vocabulario

**¿Adónde vas?** *Where are you going?*
**voy** *I'm going*

**yo prefiero** *I prefer*
**todos los** *all (the)*
**hasta luego** *so long*

# Diálogo

Complete the dialog by using expressions chosen from the following list:

¡Oh, sí! Él comprende mucho.
El perro come siempre.
Yo prefiero a mi gato. Hasta luego, Roberto.

¿Cómo se llama el gato?
Voy con mi gato Chiquito al parque.
Es un animal muy pequeño.

# 8 La descripción

## How to Describe Things in Spanish

**1** The words that follow are all adjectives. They describe the people and objects in the pictures. See if you can guess their meanings:

**grande**

**pequeño**

**bonito**

**feo**

**inteligente**

**estúpido**

**rico**

**pobre**

**viejo**

**joven**

**gordo**

**flaco**

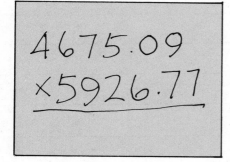

$$4675.09 \\ \times 5926.77$$

**difícil**

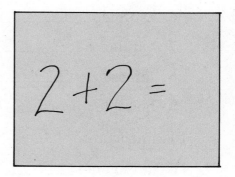

$$2 + 2 =$$

**fácil**

**moreno**

**rubio**

## Actividad A

Here is a list of Spanish adjectives that are similar to English adjectives. How many meanings can you fill in?

1. americano _____

2. confortable _____

3. delicioso _____

4. diferente _____

5. elegante _____

6. estúpido _____

7. excelente _____

8. famoso _____

9. horrible _____

10. importante _____

11. inteligente _____

12. interesante _____

13. magnífico _____

14. moderno _____

15. necesario _____

16. ordinario _____

17. perfecto _____

18. popular _____

19. romántico _____

20. tropical _____

**2** Now see if you can read and understand this story:

Manuel es un muchacho americano. Es pequeño y moreno. Es también inteligente y popular. Prefiere escuchar los discos de rock y baila muy bien. Es un muchacho perfecto.

## Actividad B
Make a list from the story of all the adjectives that describe Manuel:

1. _____     4. _____

2. _____     5. _____

3. _____     6. _____

## Actividad C
Change all the words in bold type to make the sentences true:

1. Manuel es un muchacho **español.** _____

2. Manuel es **grande** y **rubio.** _____

3. Manuel es **estúpido.** _____

4. Manuel **canta** muy bien. _____

5. Es un muchacho **ordinario.** _____

**3**  Here is another story. Can you read and understand this one, too?

Alicia es una muchacha americana. Es pequeña y
morena. Es también inteligente y popular. Es loca
por los deportes. Su deporte favorito es el tenis. Es
una muchacha perfecta.

**loca por** *crazy about*
**el deporte** *the sport*

## Actividad D
Make a list from the story of all the adjectives that describe Alicia:

1. _____    4. _____

2. _____    5. _____

3. _____    6. _____

## Actividad E
Change all the words in bold type to make the sentences true:

1. Alicia es una muchacha **española.** _____

2. Alicia es **grande** y **rubia.** _____

3. Alicia es **estúpida.** _____

4. Alicia es loca por **los muchachos.** _____

5. Es una muchacha **ordinaria.** _____

**4** Have you been observant? Look at the adjectives that describe Manuel. Compare them with the adjectives that describe Alicia. Read the adjectives aloud from left to right after your teacher:

<table>
<tr><td align="center">**Manuel**</td><td align="center">**Alicia**</td></tr>
</table>

<table>
<tr><td align="center">americano</td><td align="center">americana</td></tr>
<tr><td align="center">pequeño</td><td align="center">pequeña</td></tr>
<tr><td align="center">moreno</td><td align="center">morena</td></tr>
<tr><td align="center">rubio</td><td align="center">rubia</td></tr>
<tr><td align="center">perfecto</td><td align="center">perfecta</td></tr>
</table>

Notice that an adjective in Spanish agrees in gender with the person it describes. Which letter do the MASCULINE forms of the adjective

end in? _____ Which letter do the FEMININE forms of the adjective

end in? _____ That's right. Adjectives that end in **-o** in the MASCULINE change the **-o** ending to an **-a** ending when describing a FEMININE noun.

## Actividad F

Choose the adjective that correctly completes the sentence.

1. Enrique es _____ (rubio, rubia).

2. Carmen es _____ (rico, rica).

3. El abuelo es _____ (viejo, vieja).

4. La señora es _____ (famoso, famosa).

**5.** Pablo es _____ (moreno, morena).

**6.** La doctora es _____ (flaco, flaca).

**5** An adjective in Spanish also agrees in gender with the thing or object it describes. What letter do we change to make the MASCULINE form of the adjective FEMININE? Look carefully:

**el libro**

american**o**
modern**o**
perfect**o**
viej**o**

**la música**

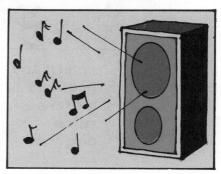

american**a**
modern**a**
perfect**a**
viej**a**

We change the letter _____ to _____.

## Actividad G

Choose the adjective that correctly describes the subject:

**1.** El tren es _____ (rápido, rápida).

**2.** La fruta es _____ (delicioso, deliciosa).

**3.** Leemos un libro _____ (romántico, romántica).

**4.** La escuela es _____ (moderno, moderna).

**5.** El automóvil es _____ (necesario, necesaria).

**6.** La música es _____ (magnífico, magnífica).

**6** Where are adjectives placed in Spanish? Usually AFTER the noun:

> **el tren *rápido***    *the fast train*
> **la fruta *deliciosa***    *the delicious fruit*

## Actividad H

Complete the sentences with the correct Spanish adjective with the proper ending:

**1.** (American)    La profesora _____ trabaja mucho.

**2.** (pretty)    La muchacha _____ baila.

**3.** (ordinary)    Yo uso una pluma _____.

**4.** (dark)    La madre es _____.

**5.** (ugly)    El tigre es _____.

**6.** (fast)    Usted usa un automóvil _____

**7.** (old)    ¿Visitas a una señora _____?

**8.** (little)    Mi gato es muy _____.

**9.** (perfect)    La profesora busca un libro _____.

**10.** (romantic)    Ella escucha la música _____.

**7**  Now look at these adjectives that could be used to describe either
Manuel or Alicia:

inteligente            inteligente
interesante            interesante
joven                  joven
pobre                  pobre
popular                popular

What do you notice about the adjectives in both columns?

_____

That's right, they do not end in **-o** or **-a.** The rule is: When an adjective ends in any letter other than **-o** in the masculine, the feminine form is the same.

There is one major exception: Most adjectives of nationality, whatever their masculine form, have feminine forms ending in **-a**:

| | | |
|---|---|---|
| **español** | **española** | *Spanish* |
| **francés** | **francesa** | *French* |
| **alemán** | **alemana** | *German* |

Examples:

| | |
|---|---|
| **el muchacho** *español* | **la muchacha** *española* |
| **el disco** *francés* | **la bicicleta** *francesa* |
| **el actor** *alemán* | **la actriz** *alemana* |

## Actividad I
Complete the sentences with the correct form of the adjective:

**1.** Pablo es popular; María es ＿＿＿＿＿＿＿＿ también.

**2.** La bicicleta es grande; el auto es ＿＿＿＿＿＿＿＿ también.

**3.** El libro es fácil; la lección es ＿＿＿＿＿＿＿＿ también.

**4.** El disco es interesante; la música es ＿＿＿＿＿＿＿＿ también.

**5.** El insecto es tropical; la fruta es ＿＿＿＿＿＿＿＿ también.

# 8

There is still more to learn about adjectives. Can you complete the second column?

I  II

| americano | americanos |
| pequeño | pequeños |
| rico | _____ |
| perfecto | _____ |
| moreno | _____ |
| elegante | _____ |
| interesante | _____ |

Look at Group I. How many people are we describing? _____

Look at Group II. How many people are we describing? _____

Which letter did we have to add to the adjective to show that we are

describing more than one? We added the letter _____.

**9**  Can you finish Group II?

I                                                II

americana                  americanas
pequeña                    pequeñas
inteligente                inteligentes

rica                       _____

perfecta                   _____

morena                     _____

elegante                   _____

interesante                _____

Look at Group I. What is the gender of the noun we are describing?

_____ How many people are we describing in Group I?

_____ Now look at Group II. How many feminine people

are we describing? _____ Which letter did we have

to add to the adjective to show that we are describing more than one?

We added the letter _____.

> Here's the rule: Adjectives in Spanish agree in GENDER and NUMBER with the person or thing they describe. If the adjective ends in a vowel, add **s** in the plural.

**10** Now complete the second column for these adjectives:

| I | II |
|---|---|
| **joven** | **jóvenes** |
| **popular** | **populares** |
| **difícil** | _____ |
| **fácil** | _____ |

Which letters did we have to add to the adjectives in Group I to show that

we are describing more than one? We added the letters _____.

> Here's the rule: If an adjective ends in a consonant, add **es** in the plural.

## Actividad J

Complete the sentences with the correct forms of the adjective:

1. La avenida es _____ (grande, grandes).

2. Mi hermana María es _____ (bonito, bonitos, bonita, bonitas).

3. Los hombres son _____ (rico, rica, ricos, ricas).

4. Las lecciones son _____ (difícil, difíciles).

5. Los árboles son _____ (tropical, tropicales).

6. El gato es un animal _____ (pequeño, pequeña, pequeños, pequeñas).

7. El señor López es un profesor _____ (inteligente, inteligentes).

8. Yo bebo un café _____ (italiano, italiana, italianos, italianas).

9. Escribo con una pluma _____ (perfecto, perfecta, perfectos, perfectas).

10. Estudio en una escuela _____ (importante, importantes).

## Actividad K

Match the expressions with the correct pictures:

el hombre viejo     el trabajo fácil
el libro importante     el animal grande
las mesas pequeñas     el muchacho pobre
la alumna popular     la señora rica
los gatos gordos     las muchachas flacas

1. _____

3. _____

2. _____

4. _____

5. _____

8. _____

6. _____

9. _____

7. _____

10. _____

## Actividad L

Fill in the correct form of the adjective in Spanish:

1. (modern)      La casa es _____.

2. (elegant)     Las mujeres son _____.

3. (difficult)   Tú contestas las preguntas _____.

4. (fast)        Los automóviles _____ pasan.

5. (old)         Comemos en un restaurante _____.

6. (important)   El español es una lengua _____.

7. (small)       Marina y Luz son niñas _____.

8. (ordinary)    La música es _____.

9. (poor)        El señor Rodríguez es _____.

10. (pretty)     Las flores son muy_____.

# Información personal

You want to join the Spanish club and are asked to give a brief description of yourself. Using some of the adjectives you have learned, write five sentences about yourself. Start each sentence with **Yo soy** *(I am):*

1. _____

2. _____

3. _____

4. _____

5. _____

# Conversación

## Vocabulario

**así, así** *so-so*
**tan** *so*
**como** *like*

**su** *her, his*
**¡Madre mía!** *My goodness!*

# Diálogo

Fill in the correct responses in the dialog. Choose from the following list:

¡Madre mía!
Así, así. ¡Qué muchacho tan magnífico!
Buenos días, señor Martínez. ¿Cómo está usted?
Y tan contento.

# Repaso II
# (Lecciones 5–8)

## Lección 5

**a.** To make a sentence negative in Spanish, that is, to say that a subject does not do something, put **no** directly before the verb:

> **Enrique *no* habla inglés.**
> **Nosotros *no* comprendemos.**

**b.** To ask a question, put the subject after the verb. An inverted question mark is placed at the beginning of a question:

> *¿Habla* **Enrique español?**
> *¿Come* **usted la fruta?**

## Lección 6

| | | | | | |
|---|---|---|---|---|---|
| 0 | cero | | | | |
| 1 | uno | 11 | once | 21 | veinte y uno |
| 2 | dos | 12 | doce | 22 | veinte y dos |
| 3 | tres | 13 | trece | 23 | veinte y tres |
| 4 | cuatro | 14 | catorce | 24 | veinte y cuatro |
| 5 | cinco | 15 | quince | 25 | veinte y cinco |
| 6 | seis | 16 | diez y seis | 26 | veinte y seis |
| 7 | siete | 17 | diez y siete | 27 | veinte y siete |
| 8 | ocho | 18 | diez y ocho | 28 | veinte y ocho |
| 9 | nueve | 19 | diez y nueve | 29 | veinte y nueve |
| 10 | diez | 20 | veinte | 30 | treinta |

$+$ **y**   $-$ **menos**   $\times$ **por**   $\div$ **divido por**   $=$ **es, son**

## Lección 7

**a.** To conjugate an **-ER** verb, drop **-ER** from the infinitive (the form of the verb before conjugation) and add the appropriate endings:

Ejemplo: **comprender**

| If the subject is | | add | to the remaining stem: |
|---|---|---|---|
| **yo** | | **o** | **yo comprendo** |
| **tú** | | **es** | **tú comprendes** |
| **usted** | | **e** | **usted comprende** |
| **él** | | **e** | **él comprende** |
| **ella** | | **e** | **ella comprende** |
| **nosotros** }  **nosotras** | | **emos** | **nosotros** } **comprendemos** **nosotras** |
| **ustedes** | | **en** | **ustedes comprenden** |
| **ellos** } **ellas** | | **en** | **ellos** } **comprenden** **ellas** |

**b.** The preposition **a** is placed before the direct object if the direct object is a person or a pet. This **a** is called the "personal **a**":

**Yo veo *a* Pablo.**
**Pedro visita *a* la muchacha.**
**Carmen ama *a* su gato.**

The combination **a** + **el** forms the contraction **al:**

**Escuchamos *al* profesor.**

## Lección 8

**a.** Adjectives agree in GENDER and NUMBER with the nouns they describe. If the noun is feminine, the adjective is feminine. If the noun is masculine, the adjective is masculine. If the noun is plural, the adjective is plural:

**la escuela moderna**     **las escuelas modernas**
**el libro americano**     **los libros americanos**

**b.** Adjectives that do not end in **-o** have the same form in the masculine and feminine, except adjectives of nationality, which have feminine forms in **-a**:

el actor *inteligente*     but     el actor *español*
la niña *inteligente*              la actriz *española*

**c.** If an adjective ends in a consonant, add **es** in the plural:

el disco popular      los discos popular*es*
la pregunta difícil    las preguntas difícil*es*

**d.** Spanish adjectives usually follow the noun.

## Actividad A

Here are nine pictures of people doing things. Complete the description below each picture by using the correct form of one of these verbs:

aprender      comer        correr      responder      ver
beber         comprender    leer       vender

1. Yo _____ agua.

2. Carmen _____ un sandwich.

3. Ellas _____ un periódico.

4. El niño no _____.

**5.** Los niños _____
en el parque.

**7.** El hombre _____
un sombrero.

**6.** Raúl _____
matemáticas.

**8.** La señorita no _____
el camello.

**9.** La muchacha _____
bien.

## Actividad B

Hidden in the puzzle below are:

| 9 adjectives | 4 verbs | 3 nouns | 2 numbers |
|---|---|---|---|
| _____ | _____ | _____ | _____ |
| _____ | _____ | _____ | _____ |
| _____ | _____ | _____ | |
| _____ | | | |

_____

Write the hidden words in the spaces above, then circle them in the puzzle. The words may be read from left to right, right to left, up or down, or diagonally:

```
A  M  U  N  D  O  D  R  O  G
M  M  O  D  E  R  N  O  B  E
O  D  E  F  D  R  I  C  O  V
L  E  E  R  V  E  R  C  N  E
F  N  R  E  I  H  A  D  I  I
Á  Í  B  M  F  C  M  O  T  N
C  D  O  O  L  P  A  S  O  T
I  R  P  C  O  S  C  N  S  E
L  A  R  E  R  R  O  C  O  X
F  J  R  U  B  I  O  F  E  O
```

# Actividad C
Crucigrama:

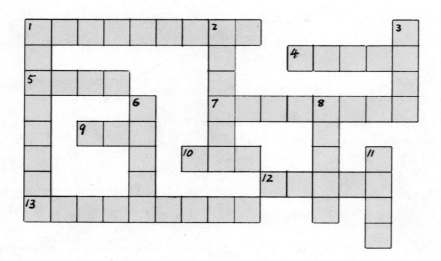

HORIZONTALES

1. American
4. nine
5. rich
7. to listen
9. ugly
10. two
12. seven
13. romantic

VERTICALES

1. to learn
2. number
3. to read
6. young
8. to eat
11. six

## Actividad D

Are you a good detective? Match the people with their descriptions:

**Micaela:** doce años, bonita, rubia, pequeña, tímida.
**Ramón:** veinte años, moreno, grande, inteligente.
**Carmen:** diez y nueve años, morena, grande, rica, elegante.
**Juanito:** quince años, rubio, pequeño, contento.

1. _____

3. _____

2. _____

4. _____

## Actividad E

Would you like to tell your future? Follow these simple rules to see what the cards have in store for you. Choose a number between two and seven. Starting in the upper left corner and moving from left to right, write down all the letters that appear under that number in Spanish:

| tres F | cuatro U | dos T | siete M | cinco C | seis V | siete U | seis I |
|---|---|---|---|---|---|---|---|
| cuatro N | seis D | dos R | dos A | seis A | tres O | cuatro A | tres R |
| dos B | siete C | tres T | dos A | siete H | tres U | cuatro U | siete O |
| cuatro T | siete S | cinco A | cuatro O | siete A | dos J | cinco S | seis C |
| cuatro M | tres N | cinco A | dos O | seis O | cinco B | tres A | cuatro O |
| dos F | tres G | seis N | tres R | cuatro D | siete M | seis T | cuatro E |
| siete I | dos Á | cuatro R | dos C | siete G | seis E | cuatro N | tres A |
| cuatro O | cinco O | siete O | cinco N | tres N | seis N | tres D | dos I |
| cinco I | seis T | siete S | tres E | seis A | cinco T | dos L | cinco A |

## Actividad F

Picture Story. Can you read this story? Much of it is in picture form. Whenever you come to a picture, read it as if it were a Spanish word:

Yo vivo en una  grande. En mi ciudad hay

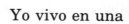 modernos,  excelentes,

 nuevos y  bonitos.

En los parques hay muchas  . Para ir a las secciones diferentes

de la  , los  y las  , los

y las  usan varios métodos de transporte. Carmen usa el

 , Jorge el  . Lupita toma un

y Raúl tiene un  pequeño. Juanito y su hermana Lolita

van a la  en  .

## Actividad G

All of the following people are saying some numbers. What are they?

1. _____

3. _____

2. _____

4. _____

**5.** _____

**6.** _____

# Tercera
## Parte

# «To be or not to be»

## The Verb **ser**; Professions and Trades

**1**

**Vocabulario**
**¿Quién es?** *(Who is it?)* **Es**

**el profesor**

**la profesora**

**el médico**

**la médica**

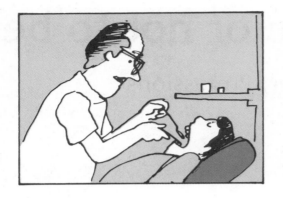

**el dentista**

**la dentista**

**el abogado**

**la abogada**

**el secretario**

**la secretaria**

**el enfermero**

**la enfermera**

**el policía**

**el cartero**

## Actividad A

Match the following occupations with the correct pictures:

**una profesora    un secretario    un médico        una abogada**
**un policía       una dentista     una enfermera    un cartero**

1. _____

2. _____

3. _____

6. _____

4. _____

7. _____

5. _____

8. _____

## Actividad B
Now identify these pictures:

1. _____

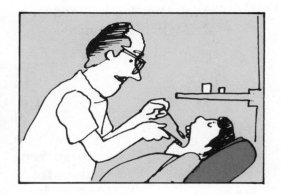

4. _____

2. _____

5. _____

3. _____

6. _____

**2**

One of the most important words in the Spanish language is the verb **ser** *(to be)*. It is irregular, that is, it doesn't follow the rules for **-er** verbs that we learned in Lesson 7. Here are the forms of **ser**. MEMORIZE them:

| | | |
|---|---|---|
| yo soy | | *I am* |
| tú eres | | *you are* (familiar) |
| Ud. es | | *you are* (formal) |
| él es | | *he is* |
| ella es | | *she is* |
| nosotros }<br>nosotras } | somos | *we are* |
| Uds. son | | *you are* (plural) |
| ellos }<br>ellas } | son | *they are* |

Before we go on, let's learn two useful abbreviations:

**Ud. = usted     Uds. = ustedes**

## Actividad C

Choose five people you know and write their professions. Write complete sentences. Note that it is not necessary to use **un** or **una**:

Example: **Trapper John es médico.**

1. _____

2. _____

3. _____

4. _____

5. _____

## Actividad D
Complete each sentence with the correct form of the verb **ser**:

1. Manuel _____ mexicano.

2. Yo _____ cartero.

3. Ella _____ secretaria.

4. ¿_____ Ud. abogado?

5. María _____ dentista.

6. Mis padres _____ médicos.

7. Ellos _____ gordos.

8. ¿_____ Uds. los hermanos de José?

9. Nosotros _____ importantes.

10. El policía _____ joven.

## Actividad E
Make all the sentences in Exercise D negative:

1. _____

2. _____

3. _____

4. _____

5. _____

6. _____

7. _____

**8.** _____

**9.** _____

**10.** _____

## Actividad F

Here are some sentences in which a form of **ser** is used. Can you match these sentences with the pictures they describe?

**Amigo es mi perro.**
**Yo soy inteligente.**
**Ella es rica.**
**Nosotras somos bonitas.**

**Tú eres moreno.**
**Ellas son flacas.**
**Ellos son pequeños.**
**Ud. es importante.**

**1.** _____

**3.** _____

**2.** _____

**4.** _____

**5.** _____

**7.** _____

**6.** _____

**8.** _____

**3** Here's a short conversation between Juanita, a new girl in school, and Mr. Fernández, the teacher of the class:

| | |
|---|---|
| EL SEÑOR FERNÁNDEZ: | Buenos días, niña. ¿Cómo te llamas? |
| JUANITA: | Me llamo Juanita Campos. |
| EL SEÑOR FERNÁNDEZ: | Juanita, ¿comprendes inglés? |
| JUANITA: | No mucho. Soy de Colombia. Hablamos español en casa. **en casa** _at home_ |
| EL SEÑOR FERNÁNDEZ: | Ah, una colombiana. ¿Tu padre está aquí? |

| | |
|---|---|
| JUANITA: | Sí, señor. |
| EL SEÑOR FERNÁNDEZ: | ¿Dónde trabaja? |
| JUANITA: | Mi padre es mecánico. Mi madre trabaja también. Es enfermera en un hospital. |
| EL SEÑOR FERNÁNDEZ: | Está bien. No hay problema. Si estudias todos los días, vas a aprender mucho en mi clase. |
| JUANITA: | Gracias, señor profesor. |
| EL SEÑOR FERNÁNDEZ: | De nada. |
| JUANITA: | Hasta mañana. |

**todos los días** *every day*
**vas** *you are going*

**de nada** *you're welcome*

## Actividad G

**¿Cierto o falso?** These statements are based on the dialog you've just read. If the statement is true, write **cierto.** If it is false, write the correct information:

1. Juanita Campos es la profesora de la clase. _____

2. El señor Fernández habla español. _____

**3.** Juanita Campos no habla inglés. _____

**4.** El padre de Juanita trabaja en un hospital. _____

**5.** Juanita es cubana. _____

**6.** La madre de Juanita no trabaja. _____

**7.** Juanita habla inglés en casa. _____

**8.** Juanita va a la escuela mañana. _____

## Actividad H
Answer the questions:

**1.** ¿Quién es Juanita Campos?

_____

**2.** ¿Qué lengua habla Juanita?

_____

**3.** ¿Habla español el señor Fernández?

_____

**4.** ¿Dónde trabaja la madre de Juanita?

_____

**5.** ¿De qué nacionalidad es Juanita?

_____

# Conversación

**Vocabulario**

**nunca** *never*
**estamos** *we are*

**enfermo** *sick*

# Preguntas personales

1. ¿Eres inteligente o estúpido (estúpida)?

   _____

2. ¿Eres grande o pequeño (pequeña)?

   _____

3. ¿Eres rubio (rubia) o moreno (morena)?

   _____

4. ¿Eres gordo (gorda) o flaco (flaca)?

   _____

# Información personal

Describe the people in these professions:

1. Un actor es _____

2. Un médico es _____

3. Una dentista es _____

4. Un profesor es _____

5. Una abogada es _____

6. Una secretaria es _____

7. Un mecánico es _____

Choose the best answers to the questions from the following list:

Yo soy alumno.  Es mi hermana.
Es actor.  No, es policía.

# 10 Más verbos

## -IR Verbs

**1** This new group of verbs belongs to the **-IR** conjugation. See if you can guess their meanings:

**abrir**

**cubrir**

**dividir**

**escribir**

**recibir**

**sufrir**

**vivir**

Here are seven more action words. Do you recall what you did with **-ar** and **-er** verbs when you used them? We dropped the **-ar** and **-er** and added certain endings. We must do the same thing with **-ir** verbs. Here's an example, using the verb **escribir** (*to write*):

| | |
|---|---|
| **yo escribo** | *I write, I am writing* |
| **tú escribes** | *you write, you are writing* (familiar) |
| **Ud. escribe** | *you write, you are writing* (formal) |
| **él escribe** | *he writes, he is writing* |
| **ella escribe** | *she writes, she is writing* |
| **nosotros** } **escribimos** **nosotras** | *we write, we are writing* |
| **Uds. escriben** | *you write, you are writing* (plural) |
| **ellos** } **escriben** **ellas** | *they write, they are writing* |

**2** If you compare the **-er** and **-ir** verbs, what do you notice? Almost all the endings are the same! The only exception is the **nosotros** form. In this form, the **-er** ending is **-emos** but the **-ir** ending is **-imos.** That makes things simple. Let's do another one. Add the proper endings:

### abrir (*to open*)

yo abr _____

tú abr _____

él abr _____

ella abr _____

nosotros⎫
nosotras⎭ abr _____

Uds. abr _____

ellos⎫
ellas⎭ abr _____

## Actividad A

Let's practice with other **-ir** verbs:

|  | cubrir | dividir | recibir | sufrir |
|---|---|---|---|---|
| yo | _____ | _____ | _____ | _____ |
| tú | _____ | _____ | _____ | _____ |
| usted | _____ | _____ | _____ | _____ |
| él | _____ | _____ | _____ | _____ |
| ella | _____ | _____ | _____ | _____ |
| nosotros | _____ | _____ | _____ | _____ |
| ustedes | _____ | _____ | _____ | _____ |
| ellos | _____ | _____ | _____ | _____ |
| ellas | _____ | _____ | _____ | _____ |

## Actividad B

Match the sentences with the pictures they describe:

Él abre la ventana.    Nosotros dividimos las frutas.
Tú vives con tu familia.    Yo recibo una bicicleta.
Ellas sufren mucho.    Ud. cubre la mesa.

1. _____

4. _____

2. _____

5. _____

3. _____

6. _____

## Actividad C

Match the Spanish verbs with the English meanings and write the matching letters in the space provided:

1. yo abro          _____

2. ellos reciben      _____

3. Uds. viven        _____

4. tú escribes       _____

5. nosotros escribimos   _____

6. él vive           _____

7. ellos cubren      _____

8. ellos viven       _____

9. ella recibe       _____

10. él divide        _____

11. Ud. cubre       _____

12. tú vives         _____

13. nosotros dividimos .   _____

14. yo escribo       _____

15. ellos abren       _____

**a.** I write
**b.** you live (plural)
**c.** they open
**d.** she receives
**e.** we divide
**f.** you cover
**g.** you write
**h.** you live (singular)
**i.** they receive
**j.** I open
**k.** we write
**l.** he lives
**m.** he divides
**n.** they live
**o.** they cover

**3**

Here's one more important **-ir** verb: **salir** (*to leave, to go out*). We present it separately because (a) it has an irregular **yo** form: **salgo;** (b) it is followed by **de** if you mention the place you're "going out of":

> **Yo *salgo* ahora.**  *I'm leaving (going out) now.*
> But:
> **Yo *salgo de* la casa ahora.**  *I'm leaving the house now.*

## Actividad D

Complete the Spanish sentences with the correct forms of **salir** and write the English meanings in the spaces provided:

1. Ellos _____ mañana.

   _____

2. Yo _____ _____ la clase.

   _____

3. Ella _____ con su perro.

   _____

4. ¿Cuándo _____ tú _____ la casa?

   _____

5. ¿_____ ustedes ahora?

   _____

6. Nosotros _____ hoy.

   _____

7. Ud. no _____ _____ la casa.

   _____

**4** Now we are ready to compare all three kinds of verbs: **-ar, -er,** and **-ir:**

|  | **pasar** | **beber** | **vivir** |
|---|---|---|---|
| yo | pas**o** | beb**o** | viv**o** |
| tú | pas**as** | beb**es** | viv**es** |
| Ud. | pas**a** | beb**e** | viv**e** |
| él | pas**a** | beb**e** | viv**e** |
| ella | pas**a** | beb**e** | viv**e** |
| nosotros }<br>nosotras } | pas**amos** | beb**emos** | viv**imos** |
| Uds. | pas**an** | beb**en** | viv**en** |
| ellos }<br>ellas } | pas**an** | beb**en** | viv**en** |

## Actividad E

Three meanings are listed below each picture. Underline the correct meaning:

**1.**
   a. yo escribo
   b. yo entro
   c. yo pregunto

**2.**
   a. él abre
   b. él baila
   c. él vende

**3.**

   a. nosotros recibimos
   b. nosotros cantamos
   c. nosotros respondemos

**4.**

   a. ellos compran
   b. ellos corren
   c. ellos usan

**5.**

   a. él sale
   b. él divide
   c. él canta

**6.**

   a. Ud. come
   b. Ud. bebe
   c. Ud. estudia

**7.**

   a. Rosita escucha
   b. Rosita abre
   c. Rosita divide

**8.**

   a. Carlos y María cubren
   b. Carlos y María viven
   c. Carlos y María entran

**9.**
  a. yo visito
  b. yo paso
  c. yo trabajo

**10.**
  a. Francisca lee
  b. Francisca aprende
  c. Francisca mira

## Actividad F

Complete each sentence with the correct form of the verb:

**1.** (salir) Yo _____ de la ciudad mañana.

**2.** (saber) Uds. _____ mucho.

**3.** (ser) Los muchachos _____ americanos.

**4.** (visitar) Yo _____ a mi amigo.

**5.** (responder) Ella _____ en la clase.

**6.** (recibir) Ellos _____ mucho dinero.

**7.** (beber) Tú _____ una soda.

**8.** (abrir) Pablo _____ la puerta.

**9.** (vivir) María y yo _____ en Chicago.

**10.** (desear) Yo _____ correr en la calle.

**5**  Here's a conversation containing **-ar, -er,** and **-ir** verbs. Paco's friends are talking about Paco's father. All of them are trying to find out what his father does for a living. Would you know?

| | |
|---|---|
| MARÍA: | ¿La familia de Paco **vive** bien? |
| ROBERTO: | Sí, ellos **viven** en una casa magnífica. |
| CARLOS: | Y tienen un automóvil nuevo. |
| ANA: | Hay dos hermanas en la familia, Carmen y Rosa. Una es enfermera, la otra es secretaria. Ellas siempre **compran** ropa bonita. |

**tienen** *they have*

**la ropa** *the clothing*

| | |
|---|---|
| ANTONIO: | Ellos **comen** y **beben** bien. Cuando yo **visito** a la familia, siempre hay mucha comida en la mesa. |
| MARÍA: | ¿Qué hace el padre de Paco? |
| | (Entra Paco.) |

**¿Qué hace . . . ?** *What does . . . do?*

| ROBERTO: | Paco, ¿dónde **trabaja** tu padre? |
| PACO: | Mi padre tiene un supermercado. |
| LOS AMIGOS: | Ahora **comprendemos** por qué hay mucha comida en tu casa. |

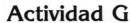

## Actividad G

Pick out the regular **-ar, -er,** and **-ir** verbs in the conversation and list them in the infinitive form:

| **-ar** verbs | **-er** verbs | **-ir** verbs |
| --- | --- | --- |
| _____ | _____ | _____ |
| _____ | _____ | |
| _____ | _____ | |

## Actividad H

Complete the sentences by choosing the correct words and writing them in the blanks:

1. María y Ana son _____ de Paco.
   a. amigos  b. hermanas  c. tías  d. amigas

2. La familia de Paco _____ una casa grande.
   a. compra  b. desea  c. vive en  d. vende

3. El automóvil de la familia es _____.
   a. grande  b. magnífico  c. viejo  d. nuevo

4. Hay _____ hermanas en la familia.
   a. dos   b. tres   c. cuatro   d. cinco

5. La enfermera trabaja probablemente en _____.
   a. el supermercado   b. la casa   c. el hospital   d. el cine

6. Carmen y Rosa son _____.
   a. hermanas   b. tías   c. abuelas   d. enfermeras

7. Una secretaria trabaja en _____.
   a. una tienda   b. una oficina   c. un teatro   d. un restaurante

8. La familia de Paco _____ bien.
   a. estudia   b. aprende   c. escucha   d. come

9. Un _____ es una persona que trabaja con los enfermos.
   a. cartero   b. abogado   c. mecánico   d. médico

10. En un supermercado no hay _____.
   a. soda   b. radios   c. frutas   d. leche

## Actividad I

Here's a story with many missing words. Can you fill all the blanks so that the story makes sense? Have fun!

La familia de Paco _____ bien. Ellos _____ en

una casa _____. Hay dos _____: Carmen y Rosa.

Una es _____ y la otra es _____. Ellas siempre

_____ ropa _____. La familia _____ y

_____ bien. Siempre hay mucha _____ en la

_____. El padre _____ en un _____.

# Conversación

## Vocabulario

**¿Qué haces?** *What are you doing?*
**con quienes** *with whom*

**tú sabes** *you know*
**(yo) sé** *I know*

# Diálogo

Choose the best response to each question:

# Información personal

Describe yourself and your family by completing these sentences:

1. Me llamo _____.

2. Soy _____.

3. Vivo _____.

4. Yo tengo (No tengo) un automóvil _____.

5. Hay _____ hermanos (hermanas) en mi familia.

6. Se llaman _____.

7. Compran ropa _____.

8. Mi padre es _____.

9. Mi padre trabaja _____ días por semana.

10. Somos una familia _____.

# ¿Cómo estás?

## Expressions with **estar**

**1** "To be or not to be?" We have already learned one verb that means *to be:* **ser.** Here's another one: **estar.**

Yo *estoy* aquí.

Tú *estás* allí.

Él *está* enfermo.

Ella *está* bien.

**Ud. *está* triste.**

**Uds. *están* cansados.**

**Nosotros *estamos* contentos.**

**Ellos *están* sentados.**

**2** Let's see how **estar** is conjugated. You can see that, like **ser, estar** is somewhat irregular:

| | |
|---|---|
| **yo estoy** | *I am* |
| **tú estás** | *you are* (familiar) |
| **Ud. está** | *you are* (formal) |
| **él está** | *he is* |
| **ella está** | *she is* |
| **nosotros** ⎫ **estamos**<br>**nosotras** ⎭ | *we are* |
| **Uds. están** | *you are* (plural) |
| **ellos** ⎫ **están**<br>**ellas** ⎭ | *they are* |

**3**

The question now is: When do we use forms of **ser** and when do we use forms of **estar**? For example, if we want to say *I am,* do we say **yo soy** or **yo estoy**? If we want to say *she is,* do we say **ella es** or **ella está**?

We can't just use whichever verb we feel like using. There are certain rules. The following examples show three special uses of the verb **estar:**

a. **¿Cómo *está* Ud.?**       *How are you?*
   **Yo *estoy* bien, gracias.**   *I'm well, thank you.*
   **No *estoy* bien; *estoy* enfermo.**  *I'm not well; I'm sick.*

Do you know why we use forms of the verb **estar** in these three sentences? The reason is that they ask or talk about a person's HEALTH.

b. **¿Dónde *está* la casa?**   *Where is the house?*
   **Madrid *está* en España.**  *Madrid is in Spain.*

In these sentences, we are telling something's or someone's LOCATION.

c. **María *está* contenta.**   *María is happy.*
   ***Estamos* cansados.**   *We are tired.*
   **La sopa *está* fría.**   *The soup is cold.*

In these sentences, you will notice that the condition of the persons or things can quickly change:

   **María *está* contenta.** (It's only how she feels right now.)
   ***Estamos* cansados.** (With a little rest, that will change.)
   **La sopa *está* fría.** (It can be heated up again in a few seconds.)

Therefore, the CONDITION of these things or persons is not permanent but temporary.

**4**

Here, then, are the simple rules. There are three situations in which we use a form of **estar:**

a. HEALTH. If we ask about or tell about someone's health:

      **Yo *estoy* bien.**   *I am well.*
      **Juan *está* enfermo.**  *Juan is sick.*

**b.** LOCATION. If we ask about or tell about where something or someone is:

**Los alumnos *están* en la clase.** *The students are in the class-room.*

**c.** TEMPORARY CONDITION. If the adjective describes a temporary condition that can change back and forth:

**El café *está* caliente.** *The coffee is warm.*
**María *está* triste.** *María is sad.*
**La puerta *está* abierta.** *The door is open.*

Now you know the three situations in which you use **estar.** In all other situations, use the verb **ser.**

NOTE: Sometimes it is not easy to decide whether a condition is "temporary" or "permanent." In Spanish, some conditions are usually regarded as permanent characteristics. Adjectives like **rico, pobre, gordo, flaco, joven,** and **viejo** are usually considered permanent characteristics. Therefore, we say in Spanish:

**Yo *soy* rico.**    **La abuela *es* vieja.**
**Mi amigo *es* pobre.**    **Los muchachos *son* gordos.**

## Actividad A

Complete the sentences with the correct forms of **estar,** then tell why you use **estar** instead of **ser:**

1. Ellos _____ en Madrid.

2. María _____ enferma.

3. Nosotros _____ contentos ahora.

4. ¿Cómo _____ Ud.?

5. ¿Cómo _____ Uds.?

6. ¿Dónde _____ mi padre?

7. La soda _____ fría.

8. Los muchachos _____ sentados en la mesa.

9. ¡Qué trabajo! Yo _____ cansado.

10. Mi hermano no _____ bien hoy.

**5** Let's review the two verbs that mean *to be*. Repeat them aloud after your teacher:

| ser | | | estar |
|---|---|---|---|
| yo soy | *I am* | | yo estoy |
| tú eres | *you are* | | tú estás |
| Ud. es | | | Ud. está |
| él es | *he is* | | él está |
| ella es | *she is* | | ella está |
| nosotros / nosotras } somos | *we are* | | nosotros / nosotras } estamos |
| Uds. son | *you are* | | Uds. están |
| ellos / ellas } son | *they are* | | ellos / ellas } están |

## Actividad B

Match the sentences with the correct pictures:

**Mi abuelo es carpintero.**
**El agua está caliente.**
**Ellas son abogadas.**

**¿Es María gorda?**
**El médico está en el hospital.**
**Nosotros somos americanos.**

1. _____     2. _____

**3.** _____  **5.** _____

**4.** _____  **6.** _____

## Actividad C

Choose between forms of **estar** and **ser**. Underline the correct form:

1. Roberto (es, está) alegre hoy.
2. Yo (soy, estoy) mexicano.
3. Ella (es, está) secretaria.
4. ¿Cómo (es, está) Ud.?
5. ¿Dónde (son, están) mis padres?
6. Uds. (son, están) inteligentes.
7. El abuelo (es, está) viejo.
8. Nosotros (somos, estamos) bien, gracias.
9. Mi profesor (es, está) joven.
10. Las casas (son, están) grandes.

**6**    Now read this story:

¡Pobre Rosita! Ella no está bien. Está en casa todo el día porque está enferma. No desea comer. No desea leer. No desea mirar la televisión. La madre de Rosita está triste también cuando ella ve a la muchacha enferma.

**todo el día** *all day*

MADRE:           ¡Mi pobre hija! Tú sufres mucho.

ROSITA:          Sí, sufro mucho, mamá. Ay, ay, ay, ¡qué dolor!

**el dolor** *the pain*

MADRE:           Mi pobre hija necesita un médico. ¿Dónde está el doctor Curante?

Entra el doctor Curante. Es joven y guapo. Él sabe mucho sobre medicina. Comprende a las muchachas también.

**sobre** *about*

EL DOCTOR CURANTE: ¿Dónde está la paciente? ¡Ajá! Aquí está la enferma. ¿Cómo estás, Rosita? ¿Por qué estás triste? Mañana es un día de fiesta. No hay clases.

el día de fiesta *the holiday*

ROSITA: ¿No hay clases? ¿Es un día de fiesta? ¡Ay, gracias! Estoy bien ahora.

## Actividad D

Complete each sentence with the correct word, based on the story you have just read:

1. Rosita no _____ bien hoy.

2. Está en _____ porque está _____.

3. Rosita _____ mucho.

4. La muchacha necesita un _____.

5. ¿Dónde _____ el doctor?

6. El doctor Curante _____ joven.

7. ¿Cómo _____, Rosita? ¿Por qué _____ triste?

8. Mañana _____ un día de fiesta.

9. No _____ clases.

10. Ahora Rosita _____ contenta.

# Conversación

## Vocabulario

**¿Qué pasa?** *What's wrong?*

**el resfriado** *the cold*

## ■ Preguntas personales

Can you give honest answers to these questions? Try your best:

**1.** ¿Estás contento (contenta) cuando hay clases?

_____

**2.** ¿Sufres mucho en la clase de español?

_____

**3.** ¿Deseas mirar la televisión todo el día?

_____

**4.** ¿Eres joven y guapo (bonita)?

_____

## ■ Información personal

The school computer is assembling a personality profile for every student. You are asked to answer the following questions truthfully:

|    |                                               | Sí | No |
|----|-----------------------------------------------|----|----|
| 1.  | ¿Eres inteligente?                           | ☐  | ☐  |
| 2.  | ¿Estás contento (contenta)?                  | ☐  | ☐  |
| 3.  | ¿Eres gordo (gorda)?                         | ☐  | ☐  |
| 4.  | ¿Estás enfermo (enferma) el día de un examen?| ☐  | ☐  |
| 5.  | ¿Eres rico (rica)?                           | ☐  | ☐  |
| 6.  | ¿Estás triste en la clase de español?        | ☐  | ☐  |
| 7.  | ¿Eres feo (fea)?                             | ☐  | ☐  |
| 8.  | ¿Estás cansado (cansada) todo el día?        | ☐  | ☐  |
| 9.  | ¿Eres joven?                                 | ☐  | ☐  |
| 10. | ¿Estás bien hoy?                             | ☐  | ☐  |

## Diálogo

Fill in the words that are missing from the dialog. Choose from the following list:

| | | | |
|---|---|---|---|
| mucho dinero | una lámpara | pasa | a la escuela |
| un resfriado | enferma | una pregunta | comer |
| muchas gracias | importante | al supermercado | bailar |
| pobre | estás | una medicina | eres |

# 12 ¿Qué hora es?

Telling Time in Spanish

**1** ¿Qué hora es?

Es la una.

Son las dos.

Son las tres.

Son las cuatro.

Son las cinco.

Son las seis.

Now see if you can do the rest:

Note that "It's 12:00 noon" can also be **Es mediodía,** and "It's 12:00 midnight" can also be **Es medianoche.**

**2**  How do you say "What time is it?" in Spanish? _____

What are the words for "it is" when saying "it is one o'clock"?

_____

What are the two words for "it is" when saying any other hour?

_____

How do you say "It is noon"? _____

How do you say "It is midnight"? _____

**3**  Now study these:

**Es la una y cinco.**

**Son las dos y cinco.**

**Son las tres y cinco.**

**Son las cuatro y cinco.**

Continue writing these times:

_____

_____

_____

_____

**4** How smart are you? How would you say:

_____

_____

_____

_____

How do you express time after the hour? _____

That's right. To express time AFTER the hour, we use **y** and add the number of minutes.

How would you say:

_____

_____

_____

**5**    Now study these:

**Es la una menos cinco.**

**Son las dos menos cinco.**

**Son las tres menos cinco.**

**Son las cuatro menos cinco.**

Continue writing these times:

_____

_____

_____

**6** How would you say:

_____

_____

How do you express time before the hour? _____

That's right. To express time BEFORE the next hour, we use **menos** and subtract the number of minutes from the next hour.

How would you express:

_____

_____

**7**  Now study these:

**Es la una y cuarto.**

**Es la una menos cuarto.**

**Son las dos y cuarto.**

**Son las dos menos cuarto.**

**Son las tres y cuarto.**

**Son las tres menos cuarto.**

**Son las cuatro y cuarto.**

**Son las cuatro menos cuarto.**

How would you express:

_____

_____

_____

_____

_____

_____

_____

_____

What is the special word for "a quarter"? _____

How do you say "a quarter after"? _____

How do you say "a quarter before"? _____

**8** Now study these:

**Es la una y media.**

**Son las dos y media.**

**Son las tres y media.**

**Son las cuatro y media.**

How would you say?

_____

_____

_____

What is the special word for "half past"? _____

How do you express "half past" the hour? _____

## Actividad A

Write out these times in numbers:

    Example: **Es la una.**    **1:00**

**1.** Son las dos menos cuarto.    _____

**2.** Son las siete y media.    _____

**3.** Son las once y diez.    _____

**4.** Son las doce y cuarto.    _____

**5.** Es la una y cuarto.    _____

**6.** Son las nueve y veinte. _____

**7.** Son las tres menos diez. _____

**8.** Son las cinco menos veinte y cinco. _____

**9.** Son las diez y trece. _____

**10.** Son las cuatro menos veinte y nueve. _____

## Actividad B
Write these times in Spanish. Begin with the Spanish equivalent of "It is":

**3:20**

1. _____

**9:55**

2. _____

**4:30**

3. _____

**10:45**

4. _____

**5.** _____

**6.** _____

**7.** _____

**8.** _____

**9.** _____

**10.** _____

## Actividad C

Here are some clocks. What time does each show?

1. _____

2. _____

3. _____

4. _____

5. _____

6. _____

**7.**

**9.** _____

**8.** _____

**10.** _____

## Actividad D

Here are some broken clocks. Each one has the minute hand missing.
Can you put it back according to the correct time?

**1.** Son las dos menos cinco.

**2.** Son las tres y diez.

**3.** Son las cuatro y veinte y cinco.

**6.** Es la una menos diez.

**4.** Son las nueve y cinco.

**7.** Son las cinco menos veinte y cinco.

**5.** Son las once y cuarto.

**8.** Son las seis menos veinte.

**9.** Son las doce menos diez.

**10.** Es mediodía.

**9**  Now that you know how to answer when someone asks **¿Qué hora es?,** how do you reply if someone asks, for example:

**¿A qué hora termina la clase?**

Here's one possible answer:

**La clase termina *a las dos*.**

If you want to express "at" a certain time, which Spanish word must

you use before the time? _____

**10**  If you want to be specific about the time of day, here is what you must do:

**Yo entro en la clase de español a las ocho *de la mañana*.**
**Yo practico la lección a la una *de la tarde*.**
**Yo miro la televisión a las nueve *de la noche*.**

How do you express "in the morning" or "A.M." in Spanish? _____

How do you express "in the afternoon" or "P.M."? _____

How do you express "in the evening" or "P.M."? _____

## Actividad E

Write out in Spanish:

**1.** 6:35 P.M. _____

**2.** 2:15 A.M. _____

**3.** 3:45 P.M _____

**4.** 7:55 A.M. _____

**5.** 10:25 P.M. _____

**6.** 5:10 P.M. _____

## Actividad F

Here are some daily activities. Write the most likely answer to the question **¿Qué hora es?**:

**a.** Es la una y media de la mañana.
**b.** Son las siete de la mañana.
**c.** Son las tres de la tarde.

**1.** _____

a. Son las nueve y media de la noche.
b. Son las cuatro de la mañana.
c. Son las siete y media de la mañana.

2. _____

a. Son las ocho y diez de la mañana.
b. Son las once de la noche.
c. Es la una y cuarto de la tarde.

3. _____

a. Son las siete de la noche.
b. Son las dos de la mañana.
c. Es mediodía.

4. _____

a. Son las tres de la tarde.
b. Son las once y media de la noche.
c. Son las dos menos veinte de la mañana.

**5.** _____

a. Son las ocho de la mañana.
b. Son las cinco y media de la tarde.
c. Son las diez de la mañana.

**6.** _____

a. Son las dos y media de la mañana.
b. Son las cuatro y cinco de la mañana.
c. Son las siete y cuarto de la noche.

**7.** _____

**a.** Son las tres de la mañana.
**b.** Son las diez menos diez de la noche.
**c.** Es la una de la tarde.

8. _____

**a.** Son las cuatro menos diez de la tarde.
**b.** Son las siete y cuarto de la noche.
**c.** Son las diez de la noche.

9. _____

**a.** Es medianoche.
**b.** Son las diez y cinco de la mañana.
**c.** Son las nueve y media de la noche.

10. _____

**11** Now read this dialog and then answer the questions that follow:

FRANCISCO: Pepe, ¿Qué hora es?
PEPE: Son las nueve y media.
ROSITA: ¿Las nueve y media? Es imposible. En      **en** *on*
mi reloj son las diez.
FRANCISCO: ¡Ay, Dios mío! Es tarde. Hay un examen
en mi clase de inglés hoy a las nueve y
media.

ROSITA: ¿Quién es tu profesor de inglés?
FRANCISCO: El señor López, ¿por qué?
ROSITA: ¡Qué suerte! El señor López está ausente      **la suerte** *the luck*
hoy.                                           **ausente** *absent*

## Actividad G

Answer the questions in Spanish:

**1.** ¿Con quién habla Francisco?

_____

**2.** En el reloj de Pepe, ¿qué hora es?

_____

**3.** ¿Qué dice Rosita?

_____

**4.** ¿En qué clase tiene Francisco un examen?

_____

**5.** ¿Por qué no hay examen hoy?

_____

# Información personal

Complete the sentences with an appropriate time:

**1.** Yo llego (*I arrive*) a la escuela a _____.

**2.** Entro en la clase de español a _____.

**3.** Hago (*I do*) mis tareas (*homework*) a _____.

**4.** Miro la televisión a _____.

**5.** Tomo la cena (*supper*) a _____.

# Conversación

## Vocabulario

**la película** *the film, movie*
**¡Caramba!** *Gosh!*

**voy** *I'm going*

# Diálogo

Fill in the words that are missing from the dialog. Choose from the following list:

| | | | |
|---|---|---|---|
| por qué | hora | película | ver |
| las cuatro y cuarto | televisión | programa | sorpresa |
| ¿qué? | ¿cómo? | también | |

# Repaso III
# (Lecciones 9–12)

## Lección 9

The verb **ser** is an irregular verb that means *to be*. All of its forms must be memorized:

yo *soy*    nosotros ⎫
tú *eres*   nosotras ⎬ *somos*

Ud. *es*          Uds. *son*

él ⎫
ella ⎬ *es*       ellos ⎫
                ellas ⎬ *son*

## Lección 10

**a.** To conjugate an **-IR** verb, drop the **-IR** from the infinitive and add the appropriate endings:

Ejemplo: **abrir**

| If the subject is | add | to the remaining stem: |
|---|---|---|
| **yo** | **o** | **yo** abr*o* |
| **tú** | **es** | **tú** abr*es* |
| **Ud.** | **e** | **usted** abr*e* |
| **él** | **e** | **él** abr*e* |
| **ella** | **e** | **ella** abr*e* |
| **nosotros** ⎫ **nosotras** ⎭ | **imos** | **nosotros** ⎫ **nosotras** ⎭ abr*imos* |
| **Uds.** | **en** | **ustedes** abr*en* |
| **ellos** ⎫ **ellas** ⎭ | **en** | **ellos** ⎫ **ellas** ⎭ abr*en* |

**b.** The verb **salir** *(to leave, to go out)* has an irregular **yo** form (**yo salgo**) and is followed by **de** before the name of a place:

Yo *salgo de* la escuela a las dos.

## Lección 11

**a.** In Spanish, there is a second verb meaning *to be:* **estar.** Forms of **estar** are irregular and must be memorized:

yo *estoy*      nosotros ⎫ *estamos*
tú *estás*       nosotras ⎭
Ud. *está*                     Uds. *están*
él ⎫ *está*           ellos ⎫ *están*
ella ⎭                     ellas ⎭

**b.** **Ser** is used when expressing permanent characteristics:

El hombre *es* viejo.
La señora *es* dentista.

**Estar** is used in expressions of health, when referring to location, and when describing a temporary condition:

La niña *está* bien.
¿Dónde *está* Roberto?
*Estamos* muy contentos.

## Lección 12

**a.** Time is expressed as follows:

| ¿Qué hora es? | *What time is it?* |
|---|---|
| Es la una. | *It's one o'clock.* |
| Son las dos. | *It's two o'clock.* |
| Son las dos y diez. | *It's 2:10.* |
| Son las dos y cuarto. | *It's 2:15.* |
| Son las dos y media. | *It's 2:30.* |
| Son las tres menos veinte. | *It's 2:40.* |

| Es mediodía. | It's 12 noon. |
| Es medianoche. | It's 12 midnight. |
| Son las seis de la mañana. | It's 6 A.M. |
| Son las cuatro de la tarde. | It's 4 P.M. |
| Son las ocho de la noche. | It's 8 P.M. |

**b.** To express "at" at specific time, use **a:**

**¿A qué hora miras tú la televisión? — A las ocho de la noche.**

## Actividad A

Unscramble these professions. Then unscramble the letters in the circles to find out what Pedro wants to be when he grows up:

D I C O M É

E T R A C R A I S E

R O T R A C E

F R E E R O M E N

Solution:

## Actividad B

Verb Game. Here are some pictures of people doing things. Describe each picture using the correct form of one of the following verbs:

abrir     recibir
cubrir    salir
dividir   sufrir
escribir  vivir

**1.** Los alumnos _____ a las tres.

**2.** Él _____ la pluma.

**3.** La profesora _____ la ventana.

**6.** Ud. _____ a una amiga.

**4.** Nosotros _____ el automóvil.

**7.** Las niñas _____ las frutas.

**5.** Tú _____ en un apartamento.

**8.** Yo _____ mucho.

## Actividad C

How many of the words describing the pictures below do you remember? Fill in the Spanish words, then read down the boxed column to find the mystery word — something most everybody likes:

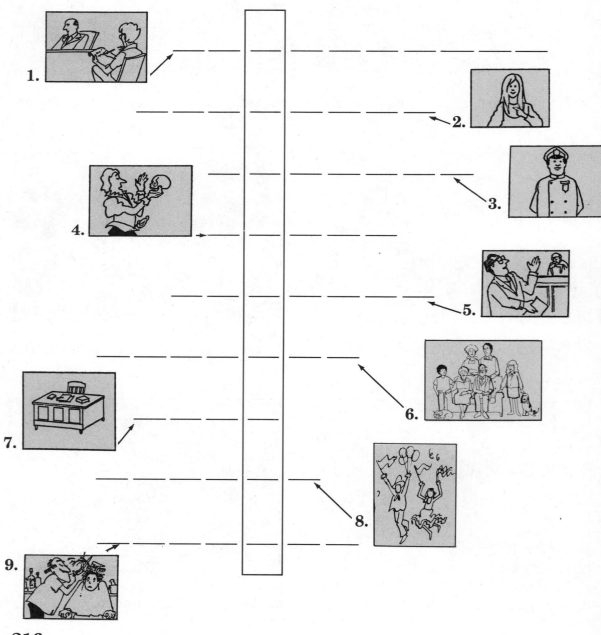

## Actividad D

Carlos could not go out of the house today. So he wrote a message in Spanish to Soledad on the window of his room. He had to write it backwards so that Soledad could read it from the street. Can you read the message? (Hint: A mirror might help.)

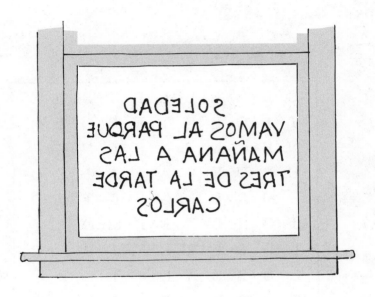

Now see if you can write a simple message in Spanish backwards. Then give it to a classmate and see if he or she can read it:

_____

_____

_____

_____

_____

## Actividad E

Word Search. There are 12 adjectives and 7 verbs hidden in the puzzle. Can you find them? The words may be read from left to right, right to left, up or down, or diagonally:

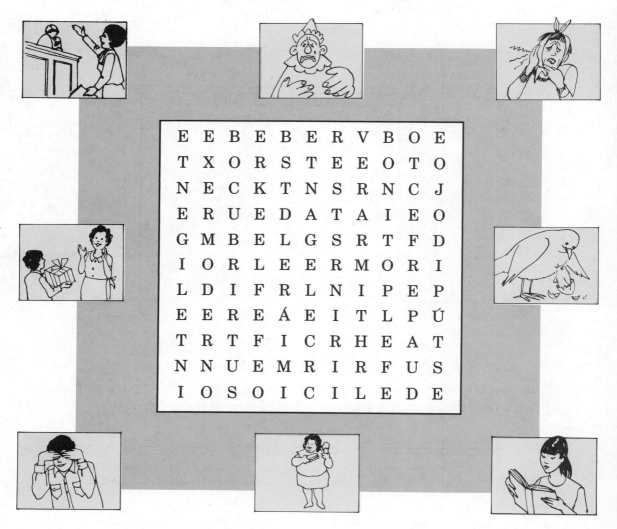

```
E E B E B E R V B O E
T X O R S T E E O T O
N E C K T N S R N C J
E R U E D A T A I E O
G M B E L G S R T F D
I O R L E E R M O R I
L D I F R L N I P E P
E E R E Á E I T L P Ú
T R T F I C R H E A T
N N U E M R I R F U S
I O S O I C I L E D E
```

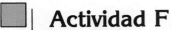

# Actividad F

Describe the pictures using forms of **estar** or **ser**:

Examples: **Él *es* alumno.**
**Ellas *están* contentas.**

1. _____

3. _____

2. _____

4. _____

**5.**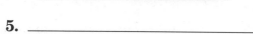

**8.** _____

**6.** _____

**9.** _____

**7.** _____

**10.** _____

## Actividad G

Picture Story. Can you read this story? Much of it is in picture form. Whenever you come to a picture, read it as if it were a Spanish word:

El señor Fernández es  en una  moderna.

Es el primer día de clases. Una  de diez años entra

en la  . Ella está muy  ; no está  .

«¿Cómo te llamas?», pregunta el 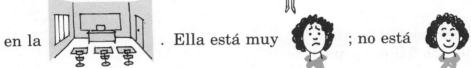 . «Me llamo Juanita»,

contesta la  . «¿Habla Ud. español?» «Sí, todos los

y todas las  de la clase hablan español.»

Ahora Juanita está  . «¿Qué hace tu padre?» pregunta el

 . «Mi padre es  y mi madre es 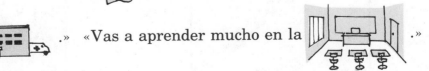 . Ella trabaja

en un  .» «Vas a aprender mucho en la 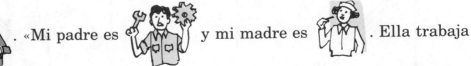 .»

«Gracias, señor profesor.»

# Achievement Test I (Lessons 1–12)

**1** Vocabulary [10 points]
Label the following pictures in Spanish:

1. _____

3. _____

2. _____

4. _____

**5.** _____

**8.** _____

**6.** _____

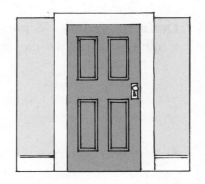

**9.** _____

**7.** _____

**10.** _____

**2**  Vocabulary [5 points]
**¿Cierto o falso?** If the statement is true, write **cierto.** If it is false, write it correctly:

1. La profesora está en la clase. _____

2. El elefante es un animal pequeño. _____

3. El médico trabaja en un banco. _____

4. Los gatos son estúpidos. _____

5. Bebemos las bananas. _____

**3**  Definite Articles [5 points]
Check whether to use **el, la, los,** or **las** with the nouns you hear:

|  | **el** | **la** | **los** | **las** |
|---|---|---|---|---|
| **1.** | _____ | _____ | _____ | _____ |
| **2.** | _____ | _____ | _____ | _____ |
| **3.** | _____ | _____ | _____ | _____ |
| **4.** | _____ | _____ | _____ | _____ |
| **5.** | _____ | _____ | _____ | _____ |

**4**  Indefinite Articles [5 points]
Check whether to use **un** or **una** with the nouns you hear:

|  | **un** | **una** |  |  | **un** | **una** |
|---|---|---|---|---|---|---|
| **1.** | _____ | _____ |  | **4.** | _____ | _____ |
| **2.** | _____ | _____ |  | **5.** | _____ | _____ |
| **3.** | _____ | _____ |  |  |  |  |

# 5 Numbers [10 points]
You will hear ten numbers in Spanish. Write them down in numerals:

1. _____    5. _____    8. _____

2. _____    6. _____    9. _____

3. _____    7. _____    10. _____

4. _____

# 6 Tú or Ud. [5 points]
You will hear the names of a person or persons. Check whether you would use **tú** or **Ud.** when speaking to these people:

|  | tú | Ud. |
| --- | --- | --- |
| 1. | _____ | _____ |
| 2. | _____ | _____ |
| 3. | _____ | _____ |
| 4. | _____ | _____ |
| 5. | _____ | _____ |

# 7 Time [10 points]
You will hear ten clock times. Draw the hands on each clock in accordance with the time you hear:

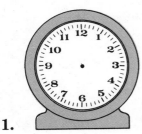

1.

2.

3.

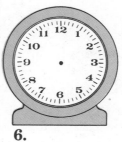

**6.**

**7.**

**9.**

**4.**

**8.**

**5.**

**10.**

## 8 Adjectives [10 points]

Write the correct forms of the Spanish adjectives:

1. the modern school     la escuela _____

2. the new car     el automóvil _____

3. the fat cats     los gatos _____

4. the pretty flowers     las flores _____

5. the blond student     la alumna _____

6. the intelligent animals     los animales _____

**7.** the small houses      las casas _____

**8.** the Spanish flag      la bandera _____

**9.** the ugly lamp      la lámpara _____

**10.** the rich doctor      el médico _____

## 9 Give the correct form of the verb [10 points]

**1.** (comprar)    Yo _____ un sombrero nuevo.

**2.** (leer)    Mi madre _____ el periódico.

**3.** (abrir)    Tú _____ los libros.

**4.** (aprender)    Ella _____ la lección.

**5.** (bailar)    Nosotros _____ la conga.

**6.** (recibir)    Ud. _____ el dinero.

**7.** (cubrir)    Él _____ la mesa.

**8.** (contestar)    María _____ la pregunta.

**9.** (ver)    Alejandro _____ la bicicleta.

**10.** (mirar)    Nosotros _____ la fotografía.

## 10 Make the following sentences negative [5 points]

**1.** La enfermera trabaja mucho.

_____

**2.** Los niños pasan.

_____

**3.** Tú hablas bien.

_____

**4.** Ella escucha la música.

_____

**5.** Ellos miran la lección.

_____

# 11 Change the statements to questions [5 points]

**6.** Usted comprende español.

_____

**7.** Ustedes bailan bien.

_____

**8.** Yo como.

_____

**9.** Tú estudias mucho.

_____

**10.** La mujer aprende.

_____

# 12 Ser and estar. Complete the sentences with the correct form of **ser** or **estar** [10 points]

**1.** ¿Cómo _____ Ud.?

**2.** Nosotros _____ aquí.

**3.** Él _____ profesor.

**4.** El café _____ caliente.

**5.** Ellos _____ abogados.

**6.** Mi amigo _____ policía.

**7.** Carlos _____ triste.

**8.** Yo _____ americana.

**9.** El parque _____ en Madrid.

**10.** Uds. _____ contentos.

## 13 Reading Comprehension [5 points]

Read the following passage and choose the expression that best completes the statement:

Carlos es un muchacho mexicano. Habla español en casa. El padre de Carlos es médico. Elena, la madre de Carlos, trabaja en una escuela grande y moderna. Carlos es alumno en una escuela pequeña. En su clase hay muchos alumnos y un profesor excelente. Hay también una pizarra, mesas y libros. Carlos trabaja mucho en la clase.

**1.** Carlos es _____ de Elena.
   (a) el hijo   (b) el hermano   (c) la hija   (d) la hermana
**2.** Carlos es
   (a) italiano   (b) mexicano   (c) americano   (d) colombiano
**3.** El padre de Carlos trabaja en
   (a) una escuela   (b) un hospital   (c) casa   (d) un cine
**4.** La madre de Carlos es
   (a) profesora   (b) dentista   (c) secretaria   (d) policía
**5.** Carlos es
   (a) popular   (b) moderno   (c) confortable   (d) inteligente

# 14 Slot Completion [5 points]

Choose the expression that best completes the sentence:

Hay una fiesta en la casa de María. Es una fiesta __(1)__. Pablo es un muchacho muy __(2)__. Él __(3)__ matemáticas y __(4)__ muy bien el español. Pablo adora a María porque ella es popular. María __(5)__ con Pablo porque es romántico.

1. (a) tropical
   (b) magnífica
   (c) morena
   (d) flaca
2. (a) necesario
   (b) rubio
   (c) interesante
   (d) estúpido
3. (a) escucha
   (b) contesta
   (c) mira
   (d) estudia
4. (a) habla
   (b) compra
   (c) ve
   (d) sale
5. (a) lee
   (b) baila
   (c) contesta
   (d) divide

# Cuarta
## Parte

# El cuerpo

## The Verb **tener**; Expressions with **tener**

**1** **El Robot**

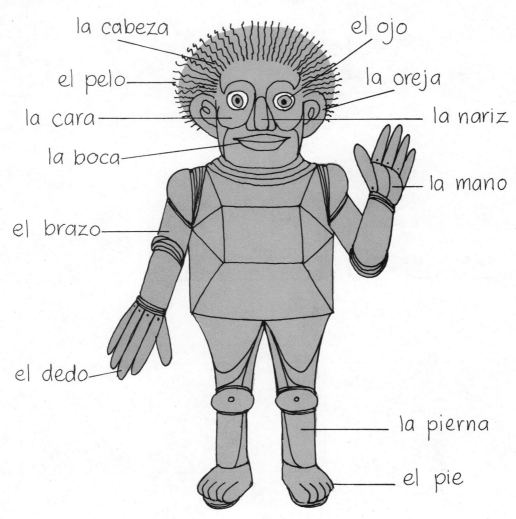

la cabeza

el ojo

el pelo

la oreja

la cara

la nariz

la boca

la mano

el brazo

el dedo

la pierna

el pie

## Actividad A

This robot may look weird, but the parts of his body are the same as yours and mine. Study them and match the Spanish words with the correct pictures:

| la boca | el dedo | la oreja |
|---------|---------|----------|
| el brazo | la mano | el pelo |
| la cabeza | la nariz | el pie |
| la cara | los ojos | la pierna |

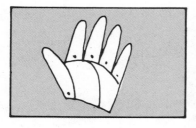

1. _____

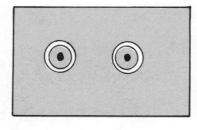

4. _____

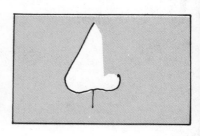

7. _____

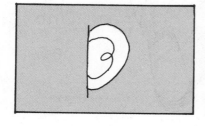

2. _____

5. _____

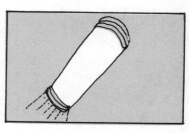

8. _____

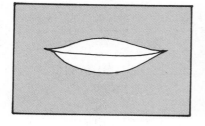

3. _____

6. _____

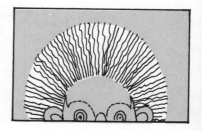

9. _____

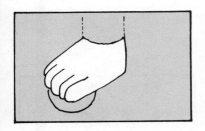

10. _____

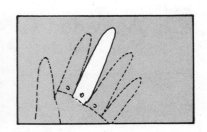

11. _____

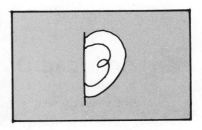

12. _____

 ## Actividad B

Label these parts of the face:

1. _____

3. _____

5. _____

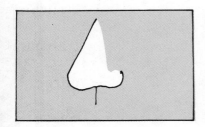

2. _____

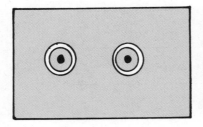

4. _____

6. _____

## Actividad C

Now label some other parts of the body:

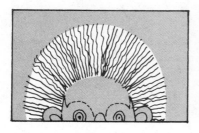

**1.** _____

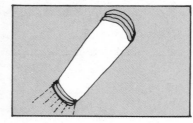

**3.** _____

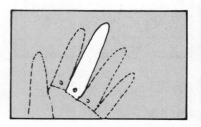

**5.** _____

**2.** _____

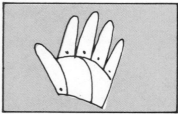

**4.** _____

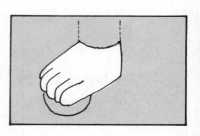

**6.** _____

## Actividad D

Every part of the body can do something. Now match the part of the body with the action it can perform. Write the matching verb in the space provided:

**1.** los ojos      _____                hablar

**2.** las piernas   _____                escribir

**3.** las manos     _____                escuchar

**4.** la boca       _____                trabajar

**5.** los pies      _____                mirar

**6.** las orejas    _____                correr

**7.** los dedos     _____                bailar

**2** Now that you are an expert on the parts of the body, you are ready to read the amazing story of Dr. Tristán Transformador, his associate, Carlota, and their wonderful creation. In this story are all the forms of the irregular Spanish verb **tener** (*to have*). See if you can find them all:

| | |
|---|---|
| LUGAR: | Un laboratorio en el pueblo de Transformia. Todos los habitantes están muy tristes porque su dictador, Decepcionador, es horrible. |
| PERSONAJES: | El doctor Tristán Transformador y su socia, Carlota. |
| EL DOCTOR: | Mi león, Feroz, está enfermo. **Tiene** una enfermedad muy seria. No puede combatir más a nuestro horrible dictador. Todos los habitantes **tienen** miedo. |

**lugar** *place*
  **el pueblo** *the town*
**los habitantes** *the inhabitants*

**personajes** *characters*
**su socia** *his associate*
**una enfermedad** *a sickness*
  **no puede . . . más** *he can no longer*
**combatir** *to fight*
  **nuestro** *our*
**tienen miedo** *are afraid*

El cuerpo   **237**

| CARLOTA: | **Tengo** una idea fantástica. **Tenemos** a Feroz en el laboratorio, ¿cierto? | **¿cierto?** *don't we?, right?* |
| EL DOCTOR: | **¿Tienes** a Feroz aquí? | |
| CARLOTA: | Sí. ¡A trabajar! Vamos a transformar el cuerpo de Feroz en un cuerpo de Autómata, un robot superior, capaz de destruir a Decepcionador. Es muy fácil. | **vamos** *we're going*<br><br>**capaz** *capable* |

|                | ¡Mira! Transformo la cabeza, la cara, |                          |
|----------------|---------------------------------------|--------------------------|
|                | los ojos, las orejas, las manos, los dedos, |                    |
|                | las piernas y los pies. ¡Aquí **tenemos** a |                    |
|                | Autómata!                             |                          |
| EL DOCTOR:     | ¡Estupendo! ¡Mira! Él quiere hablar.  | **estupendo** *marvelous,* |
| AUTÓMATA:      | Yo soy Autómata. Yo soy superior.     | *terrific*               |
| CARLOTA:       | Es cierto. Un robot superior.         | **quiere** *wants to*    |
| EL DOCTOR:     | ¡Qué robot tan estupendo! ¡Qué grande |                          |
|                | y feo! Él se parece a ＿＿＿＿＿＿       | **se parece a** *resembles* |
|                | *(Fill in someone's name — someone who* |                        |
|                | *won't get too angry with you).*      |                          |

## Actividad E

**¿Cierto o falso?** If the sentence is incorrect, change it to make it correct:

**1.** Es un laboratorio en **la ciudad de Madrid.**

＿＿＿＿＿＿＿＿＿＿＿＿＿＿＿＿＿＿＿＿＿＿＿＿＿＿＿＿.

**2.** Todos los habitantes están **contentos.**

＿＿＿＿＿＿＿＿＿＿＿＿＿＿＿＿＿＿＿＿＿＿＿＿＿＿＿＿.

**3.** **El doctor** no puede combatir más al dictador.

＿＿＿＿＿＿＿＿＿＿＿＿＿＿＿＿＿＿＿＿＿＿＿＿＿＿＿＿.

**4.** **Decepcionador** tiene una idea fantástica.

＿＿＿＿＿＿＿＿＿＿＿＿＿＿＿＿＿＿＿＿＿＿＿＿＿＿＿＿.

**5.** Carlota transforma el cuerpo de Feroz en **Autómata.**

＿＿＿＿＿＿＿＿＿＿＿＿＿＿＿＿＿＿＿＿＿＿＿＿＿＿＿＿.

**6.** Autómata es capaz de destruir **el mundo.**

＿＿＿＿＿＿＿＿＿＿＿＿＿＿＿＿＿＿＿＿＿＿＿＿＿＿＿＿.

**7.** Autómata quiere **bailar.**

_____

**8.** Autómata se parece a **Carlota.**

_____

 ## Actividad F

Fill in the names of the labeled parts of the body:

**3**  Did you find the forms of the irregular verb **tener** in our story? Here are the conjugated forms of **tener**. MEMORIZE them:

| | |
|---|---|
| **yo tengo** | *I have* |
| **tú tienes** | *you have* |
| **Ud. tiene** | *you have* |
| **él tiene** | *he has* |
| **ella tiene** | *she has* |
| **nosotros** } **tenemos**<br>**nosotras** | *we have* |
| **Uds. tienen** | *you have* |
| **ellos** } **tienen**<br>**ellas** | *they have* |

## Actividad G

Fill in the correct subject pronoun:

1. _____ tenemos los ojos azules (*blue*).

2. _____ tienen el pelo rubio.

3. _____ tengo la cara bonita.

4. _____ tiene la nariz grande.

5. _____ tienes la boca pequeña.

## Actividad H

Here are some sentences in which a form of **tener** is used. Can you match these sentences with the pictures they describe?

El robot tiene dos cabezas.
Tenemos los ojos pequeños.
Tengo diez dedos.
Ella tiene el pelo largo.
Ud. tiene las piernas largas.
No tienen pelo.

Él tiene los brazos fuertes
(*strong*).
Ellas tienen la cara bonita.
Tú tienes una boca grande.
Ud. tiene la nariz grande.

1. _____

3. _____

2. _____

4. _____

**5.** _____

**8.** _____

**6.** _____

**9.** _____

**7.** _____

**10.** _____

## Actividad I

Fill in the correct form of the verb **tener:**

1. Ellas _____ el pelo largo.

2. María _____ los ojos azules.

3. Ud. _____ las manos pequeñas.

4. Yo _____ el pelo rubio.

5. Nosotros _____ los brazos fuertes.

6. Tú _____ las orejas grandes.

7. Uds. _____ los ojos bonitos.

8. Pedro _____ los pies cansados.

## Actividad J

Make all sentences in Exercise I negative:

1. _____.

2. _____.

3. _____.

4. _____.

5. _____.

6. _____.

7. _____.

8. _____.

## Actividad K

Change all sentences in Exercise I to questions:

1. _____

2. _____

3. _____

4. _____

5. _____

6. _____

7. _____

8. _____

**4** More about **tener**. There are some very common expressions in Spanish that use the verb **tener.** The comparable English expressions use the verb "to be":

| | |
|---|---|
| **tener calor** | *to be warm* |
| **tener frío** | *to be cold* |
| **tener hambre** | *to be hungry* |
| **tener sed** | *to be thirsty* |
| **tener razón** | *to be right* |
| **no tener razón** | *to be wrong* |
| **tener sueño** | *to be sleepy* |
| **tener _____ años** | *to be _____ years old* |

Examples: **Nosotros tenemos hambre.** *We are hungry.*
**Ella tiene sed.** *She is thirsty.*

NOTE: These expressions are used only if the subject is a person. For objects (including liquids), use the verb **estar**:

**El café *está* caliente.**   *The coffee is warm.*
**Las sodas *están* frías.**   *The sodas are cold.*

## Actividad L
Label the pictures:

**Tienes doce años.**   **Tienen calor.**
**Tengo hambre.**   **Tiene frío.**
**Tenemos sed.**   **El niño tiene sueño.**

1. _____

3. _____

2. _____

4. _____

5. _____    6. _____

## Actividad M

Circle the English expression that is equivalent to the Spanish expression:

1. Tengo mucha sed.
   (a) I am very hungry.     (b) I am very thirsty.     (c) You are very tired.     (d) You are very right.

2. Él no tiene razón.
   (a) They aren't right.     (b) He is wrong.     (c) He isn't wrong.     (d) She is right.

3. ¿Tiene ella catorce años?
   (a) Is she 14 years old?     (b) He isn't 40 years old.     (c) Isn't she 14 years old?     (d) Is he 4 years old?

4. ¡No tienes razón!
   (a) You are right!     (b) You're not wrong!     (c) You are wrong!     (d) Aren't you wrong?

## Actividad N

Match the Spanish expressions with the English meanings. Write the matching letter in the space provided;

1. Tiene hambre. _____
2. Ud. tiene sed. _____
3. Tienes frío. _____
4. Tenemos calor. _____
5. Tienen trece años. _____
6. Tengo sueño. _____
7. Tienen razón. _____
8. No tiene razón. _____
9. ¿Cuántos años tienes? _____
10. ¿Tienen Uds. hambre? _____

a. You are thirsty.
b. We are hot.
c. I am sleepy.
d. They are 13 years old.
e. They are wrong.
f. Are you hungry?
g. How old are you?
h. He is hungry.
i. You are cold.
j. She is wrong.
k. They are right.
l. It is hot.

## Actividad O

Write in Spanish:

1. I am hungry. _____
2. You (*fam.*) are sleepy. _____
3. They are cold. _____
4. We are right. _____
5. You (*formal*) are thirsty. _____

# Conversación

## Vocabulario

**¿Qué te pasa?** *What's the matter?*
**tener dolor de** *to have a pain in, to have
   a(n)* _____ *ache*
**la garganta** *the throat*

**dolor de oído** *earache*
**la gripe** *the flu*
**Creo que no.** *I don't think so.*
**entonces** *well, then*

# Diálogo

Identify yourself with the person in each picture as you answer the question **¿Qué te pasa?**

1. _____

3. _____

2. _____

4. _____

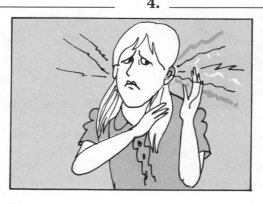

5. _____

# Preguntas personales

1. ¿Cuántos años tienes?

_____

2. ¿Tienes hambre?

_____

3. ¿Tienes siempre razón?

_____

4. ¿A qué hora tienes sueño?

_____

# Información personal

Draw your own robot creation and label the parts of the robot's body.
Then write three sentences describing the robot.

1. _____

2. _____

3. _____

# 14 Los días, los meses, las estaciones

## 1987

| | ENERO | | | | | FEBRERO | | | | | MARZO | | | |
|---|---|---|---|---|---|---|---|---|---|---|---|---|---|---|
| LUNES | | 5 | 12 | 19 | 26 | | 2 | 9 | 16 | 23 | | 2 | 9 | 16 | 23 | 30 |
| MARTES | | 6 | 13 | 20 | 27 | | 3 | 10 | 17 | 24 | | 3 | 10 | 17 | 24 | 31 |
| MIÉRCOLES | | 7 | 14 | 21 | 28 | | 4 | 11 | 18 | 25 | | 4 | 11 | 18 | 25 |
| JUEVES | 1 | 8 | 15 | 22 | 29 | | 5 | 12 | 19 | 26 | | 5 | 12 | 19 | 26 |
| VIERNES | 2 | 9 | 16 | 23 | 30 | | 6 | 13 | 20 | 27 | | 6 | 13 | 20 | 27 |
| SÁBADO | 3 | 10 | 17 | 24 | 31 | | 7 | 14 | 21 | 28 | | 7 | 14 | 21 | 28 |
| DOMINGO | 4 | 11 | 18 | 25 | | 1 | 8 | 15 | 22 | | 1 | 8 | 15 | 22 | 29 |

| | ABRIL | | | | | MAYO | | | | | JUNIO | | | |
|---|---|---|---|---|---|---|---|---|---|---|---|---|---|---|
| LUNES | | 6 | 13 | 20 | 27 | | 4 | 11 | 18 | 25 | 1 | 8 | 15 | 22 | 29 |
| MARTES | | 7 | 14 | 21 | 28 | | 5 | 12 | 19 | 26 | 2 | 9 | 16 | 23 | 30 |
| MIÉRCOLES | 1 | 8 | 15 | 22 | 29 | | 6 | 13 | 20 | 27 | 3 | 10 | 17 | 24 |
| JUEVES | 2 | 9 | 16 | 23 | 30 | | 7 | 14 | 21 | 28 | 4 | 11 | 18 | 25 |
| VIERNES | 3 | 10 | 17 | 24 | | 1 | 8 | 15 | 22 | 29 | 5 | 12 | 19 | 26 |
| SÁBADO | 4 | 11 | 18 | 25 | | 2 | 9 | 16 | 23 | 30 | 6 | 13 | 20 | 27 |
| DOMINGO | 5 | 12 | 19 | 26 | | 3 | 10 | 17 | 24 | 31 | 7 | 14 | 21 | 28 |

| | JULIO | | | | | AGOSTO | | | | | SEPTIEMBRE | | | |
|---|---|---|---|---|---|---|---|---|---|---|---|---|---|---|
| LUNES | | 6 | 13 | 20 | 27 | | 3 | 10 | 17 | 24 | 31 | | 7 | 14 | 21 | 28 |
| MARTES | | 7 | 14 | 21 | 28 | | 4 | 11 | 18 | 25 | | 1 | 8 | 15 | 22 | 29 |
| MIÉRCOLES | 1 | 8 | 15 | 22 | 29 | | 5 | 12 | 19 | 26 | | 2 | 9 | 16 | 23 | 30 |
| JUEVES | 2 | 9 | 16 | 23 | 30 | | 6 | 13 | 20 | 27 | | 3 | 10 | 17 | 24 |
| VIERNES | 3 | 10 | 17 | 24 | 31 | | 7 | 14 | 21 | 28 | | 4 | 11 | 18 | 25 |
| SÁBADO | 4 | 11 | 18 | 25 | | 1 | 8 | 15 | 22 | 29 | | 5 | 12 | 19 | 26 |
| DOMINGO | 5 | 12 | 19 | 26 | | 2 | 9 | 16 | 23 | 30 | | 6 | 13 | 20 | 27 |

| | OCTUBRE | | | | | NOVIEMBRE | | | | | DICIEMBRE | | | |
|---|---|---|---|---|---|---|---|---|---|---|---|---|---|---|
| LUNES | | 5 | 12 | 19 | 26 | | 2 | 9 | 16 | 23 | 30 | | 7 | 14 | 21 | 28 |
| MARTES | | 6 | 13 | 20 | 27 | | 3 | 10 | 17 | 24 | | 1 | 8 | 15 | 22 | 29 |
| MIÉRCOLES | | 7 | 14 | 21 | 28 | | 4 | 11 | 18 | 25 | | 2 | 9 | 16 | 23 | 30 |
| JUEVES | 1 | 8 | 15 | 22 | 29 | | 5 | 12 | 19 | 26 | | 3 | 10 | 17 | 24 | 31 |
| VIERNES | 2 | 9 | 16 | 23 | 30 | | 6 | 13 | 20 | 27 | | 4 | 11 | 18 | 25 |
| SÁBADO | 3 | 10 | 17 | 24 | 31 | | 7 | 14 | 21 | 28 | | 5 | 12 | 19 | 26 |
| DOMINGO | 4 | 11 | 18 | 25 | | 1 | 8 | 15 | 22 | 29 | | 6 | 13 | 20 | 27 |

252

**1**  Los días de la semana:

**el lunes    el miércoles   el viernes   el domingo**
**el martes   el jueves      el sábado**

NOTE: In Spanish, the days of the week are all masculine and begin
with a small letter.

---

**Un poema**

**Lunes, martes, miércoles, tres;**
**jueves, viernes, sábado, seis.**
**Y el domingo, el siete es.**

---

## Actividad A
Fill in the name of the day of the week:

1. __ o __ in __ o

2. j __ __ v __ __

3. __ á __ a __ o

4. m __ __ __ __ s

5. m __ __ r __ __ l __ __

6. __ i __ r __ e __

7. __ u __ e __

## Actividad B
Fill in the day before and after the day given:

1. _____ martes _____

2. _____ jueves _____

3. _____ sábado _____

4. _____ lunes _____

**2**    Now you can read this story about the days of the week:

**¿Cuál es tu día favorito? ¿Por qué?**

PÍA:          El viernes. Quiero ver una película con
                  mis amigas.

CARLOS:     El sábado. Tengo siempre un match de
                  tenis con mi amigo.

JOSÉ:         El domingo. Quiero mirar el fútbol en
                  la televisión.

VICTORIA: El lunes, el martes, el miércoles, el
jueves, el viernes, el sábado y el domingo.
Me gustan todos los días. Estoy siempre
contenta.

GUADALUPE: El miércoles. Tengo una clase especial
después de las clases en la escuela.       **después de** *after*
Trabajo con los computadores.

ANDRÉS: El sábado y el domingo. Me gusta           **me gusta** *I like*
dormir.                                            **dormir** *to sleep*

Los días, los meses, las estaciones     **255**

## Actividad C

Match the person with his/her favorite day or days. Write the matching letter in the space provided:

1. Andrés _____
2. José _____
3. Victoria _____
4. Carlos _____
5. Pía _____
6. Guadalupe _____

a. el sábado

b. el viernes

c. el miércoles

d. el sábado y el domingo

e. el domingo

f. el lunes, el martes, el miércoles, el jueves, el viernes, el sábado, el domingo

## Actividad D

Write in Spanish why each person prefers his/her favorite day:

1. Carlos _____

2. Victoria _____

3. Guadalupe _____

4. Pía _____

5. Andrés _____

6. José _____

## Actividad E

¿Cuál es tu día favorito? _____

¿Por qué? _____

**3** Los meses

enero

febrero

marzo

abril

mayo

junio

**julio**

**agosto**

**septiembre**

**octubre**

**noviembre**

**diciembre**

## Actividad F

Complete the names of the months:

1. __ ep __ __ e __ b __ __        7. j __ __ i __

2. __ __ __ o                      8. a __ __ __ l

3. __ i __ __ __ m __ __ e         9. f __ b __ __ __ o

4. __ u __ __ o                    10. a __ __ s __ o

5. __ o __ __ e __ b __ e          11. __ c __ u __ r __

6. m __ r __ __                    12. __ n __ __ o

## Actividad G

Fill in the months before and after the month given:

1. _____ agosto _____

2. _____ noviembre _____

3. _____ febrero _____

4. _____ mayo _____

5. _____ septiembre _____

6. _____ diciembre _____

7. _____ marzo _____

8 _____ junio _____

**4** Las cuatro estaciones:

| la primavera | el otoño |
|---|---|
| el verano | el invierno |

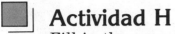 **Actividad H**

Fill in the names of the months for each season:

| la primavera | el verano | el otoño | el invierno |
|---|---|---|---|
| m_____ | j _____ | s _____ | d_____ |
| a _____ | j _____ | o _____ | e_____ |
| m_____ | a _____ | n _____ | f _____ |

## Actividad I
Identify the season:

1. _____

2. _____

3. _____     4. _____

**5**    Now you can read this story about the months of the year.

**¿Cuál es tu estación favorita? ¿Cuál es tu mes favorito? ¿Por qué?**

| | |
|---|---|
| FELIPE: | El verano. En julio me gusta ir a la playa. |
| LUISA: | El invierno. En diciembre me gusta la Navidad. |
| ROBERTO: | El otoño. En octubre quiero jugar al fútbol. |
| RODRIGO: | La primavera. En abril me gusta ir al parque. |
| GABRIELA: | El invierno. En enero quiero esquiar. |
| MÓNICA: | El otoño. En septiembre me gustan mis clases en la escuela. |
| MARÍA: | La primavera. En mayo me gustan las flores bonitas. |
| FRANCISCO: | El verano. En julio y agosto me gustan las vacaciones. |

**la playa** *the beach*

**la Navidad** *Christmas*
**jugar** *to play*

**esquiar** *to ski*

## Actividad J

Match the person with his/her favorite month. Write the matching letter in the space provided:

1. Roberto  _____

2. Mónica  _____

3. Rodrigo  _____

4. Luisa  _____

5. Francisco  _____

6. Gabriela  _____

7. María  _____

8. Felipe  _____

**a.** mayo

**b.** enero

**c.** diciembre

**d.** abril

**e.** julio

**f.** octubre

**g.** julio y agosto

**h.** septiembre

# Actividad K

Identify with each person in the story and write in Spanish why you prefer a particular month:

1. María _____

2. Francisco _____

3. Luisa _____

4. Felipe _____

5. Roberto _____

6. Mónica _____

7. Gabriela _____

8. Rodrigo _____

# Actividad L

¿Cuál es tu estación favorita? _____

¿Por qué? _____

¿Cuál es tu mes favorito? _____

¿Por qué? _____

# Actividad M

Name the season for each month:

1. abril _____     3. diciembre _____

2. junio _____     4. octubre _____

**5.** mayo _____   **9.** marzo _____

**6.** agosto _____   **10.** julio _____

**7.** septiembre _____   **11.** noviembre _____

**8.** febrero _____   **12.** enero _____


**6** Now let's see how the date is expressed in Spanish:

**¿Cuál es la fecha de hoy?**   (*What is today's date?*)

| ABRIL | | | |
|---|---|---|---|
|   | 6 | 13 | 20 | 27 |
|   | 7 | 14 | 21 | 28 |
| 1 | 8 | 15 | 22 | 29 |
| ② | 9 | 16 | 23 | 30 |
| 3 | 10 | 17 | 24 |   |
| 4 | 11 | 18 | 25 |   |
| 5 | 12 | 19 | 26 |   |

**Es el dos de abril.**

| JULIO | | | |
|---|---|---|---|
|   | 6 | 13 | 20 | 27 |
|   | 7 | 14 | 21 | 28 |
| 1 | 8 | 15 | 22 | 29 |
| 2 | 9 | 16 | 23 | 30 |
| 3 | 10 | 17 | 24 | 31 |
| 4 | ⑪ | 18 | 25 |   |
| 5 | 12 | 19 | 26 |   |

**Es el once de julio.**

| SEPTIEMBRE | | | |
|---|---|---|---|
|   | 7 | 14 | ㉑ | 28 |
| 1 | 8 | 15 | 22 | 29 |
| 2 | 9 | 16 | 23 | 30 |
| 3 | 10 | 17 | 24 |   |
| 4 | 11 | 18 | 25 |   |
| 5 | 12 | 19 | 26 |   |
| 6 | 13 | 20 | 27 |   |

**Es el veinte y uno de septiembre.**

| DICIEMBRE | | | |
|---|---|---|---|
|   | 7 | 14 | 21 | 28 |
| 1 | 8 | 15 | 22 | 29 |
| 2 | 9 | 16 | 23 | ㉚ |
| 3 | 10 | 17 | 24 | 31 |
| 4 | 11 | 18 | 25 |   |
| 5 | 12 | 19 | 26 |   |
| 6 | 13 | 20 | 27 |   |

**Es el treinta de diciembre.**

Can you fill in the blanks? To express the date, use:

**Es** + _____ + _____ + _____ + _____ .

There is just one exception: **¿Cuál es la fecha de hoy?**

| ENERO | | | |
|---|---|---|---|
| 5 | 12 | 19 | 26 |
| 6 | 13 | 20 | 27 |
| 7 | 14 | 21 | 28 |
| (1) 8 | 15 | 22 | 29 |
| 2 9 | 16 | 23 | 30 |
| 3 10 | 17 | 24 | 31 |
| 4 11 | 18 | 25 | |

**Es el primero de enero.**

To express the date when speaking of the first day of the month use:

**Es** + _____ + _____ + _____ + _____ .

If you want to include the day of the week: **Es lunes, el tres de mayo:**

**Es** + _____ + _____ + _____ + _____ + _____ .

## Actividad N

Express these dates in Spanish:

1. June 4 _____

2. January 11 _____

3. May 15 _____

4. December 21 _____

5. September 27 _____

**6.** April 30 _____

**7.** Tuesday, February 14 _____

**8.** Thursday, August 7 _____

**9.** Sunday, March 31 _____

**10.** Monday, November 1 _____

**11.** Wednesday, July 16 _____

**12.** Saturday, October 13 _____

## Actividad O

Give the dates in Spanish for these important events:

**1.** your birthday _____

**2.** Independence Day _____

**3.** Thanksgiving Day _____

**4.** Christmas _____

**5.** your favorite day of the year _____

# Conversación

## Vocabulario

**el cumpleaños** *the birthday*
**¡Qué suerte!** *What luck!*
**celebrar** *to celebrate*

**voy** *I go*
**ceno** *I dine*
**no pienso en** *I don't think of*

# Diálogo

You are the second person in the dialog. Write an original response to each dialog line following the directions given:

¿Cuál es tu mes favorito?     _____
(Tell which one.)

¿Por qué te gusta ese mes?     _____
(Tell why.)

Yo prefiero el mes de agosto.
Es el mes de mi cumpleaños.     _____
(Ask how the other person celebrates his or her birthday.)

Invito a mis amigos a una
fiesta. No pienso en la
escuela.     _____
(Give your reaction.)

# Información personal

1. ¿Cuál es la fecha de hoy?

_____

2. ¿Cuál es la fecha de tu cumpleaños?

_____

3. ¿Cuál es tu estación favorita?

_____

4. ¿En qué estación tienes frío?

_____

5. ¿En qué estación tienes calor?

_____

# Plan de la semana

List the things you plan to do for the week so that you won't forget:
Examples: **Voy a la escuela.**

        **Visitamos a los abuelos.**

        And so on.

| | |
|---|---|
| **LUNES**<br>Fecha _____ | _____<br>_____ |
| **MARTES**<br>Fecha _____ | _____<br>_____ |
| **MIÉRCOLES**<br>Fecha _____ | _____<br>_____ |
| **JUEVES**<br>Fecha _____ | _____<br>_____ |
| **VIERNES**<br>Fecha _____ | _____<br>_____ |
| **SÁBADO**<br>Fecha _____ | _____<br>_____ |
| **DOMINGO**<br>Fecha _____ | _____<br>_____ |

# Es mi casa

## Possessive Adjectives

**1** Look at the pictures and try to guess the meanings of the words:

**la casa**

**el apartamento**

**la cocina**

**el comedor**

**el cuarto de baño**

**la sala**

**el dormitorio**

**la cama**

**la mesa**

**la lámpara**

la silla

el sofá

## Actividad A
Label the pictures. Use the article **el** or **la:**

1. _____

3. _____

2. _____

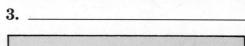

4. _____

**5.** _____

**8.** _____

**6.** _____

**9.** _____

**7.** _____

**10.** _____

## Actividad B

You have just moved into a big new house. The movers are showing you some of your things. Tell them where to put them:

Example: **en el dormitorio**

1. _____

4. _____

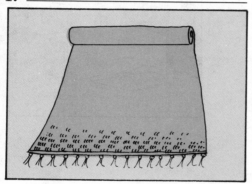

2. _____

5. _____

3. _____

6. _____

7. _____

10. _____

8. _____

11. _____

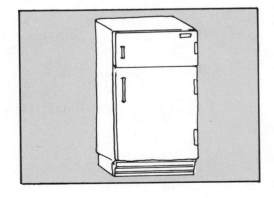

9. _____

12. _____

**2**

In this lesson you are going to learn how to say that something belongs to someone. You will learn about possession and possessive adjectives. Pay special attention to each group of sentences:

| I | II |
|---|---|
| Es *mi* perro. | Son *mis* perros. |
| Es *mi* amiga. | Son *mis* amigas. |

Look at the nouns in Group I. Underline them.

Are these nouns singular or plural? _____

What does **mi** mean? _____

Now look at Group II. Which word has replaced **mi** from Group I?

_____ What does **mis** mean? _____

Here's the rule: There are two words in Spanish for *my*. **Mi** is used when the noun is singular; **mis** is used when the noun is plural.

## Actividad C
Complete with **mi** or **mis**:

1. _____ hermano

2. _____ casas

3. _____ pluma

4. _____ amigas

5. _____ libros

6. _____ discos

7. _____ gato

8. _____ televisión

9. _____ sillas

10. _____ dormitorio

## Actividad D
Complete the sentences:

1. La madre de mi padre es _____.

**2.** La hija de mi madre es _____.

**3.** La madre de mi madre es _____.

**4.** Los hijos de mis padres son _____.

**5.** Los padres de mi padre son _____.

**3** See if you can apply the rule you have learned to other possessive adjectives:

<table>
<tr><td>I</td><td>II</td></tr>
<tr><td>Es tu gato.</td><td>Son tus gatos.</td></tr>
<tr><td>Es tu pluma.</td><td>Son tus plumas.</td></tr>
</table>

What do **tu** and **tus** mean? _____

When do you use **tu?** _____

When do you use **tus?** _____

When you use **tu** or **tus,** are you being familiar or formal? _____

## Actividad E
Complete with **tu** or **tus:**

**1.** _____ escuela

**2.** _____ padre

**3.** _____ profesores

**4.** _____ abuelos

**5.** _____ bicicleta

**6.** _____ clases

**7.** _____ lámpara

**8.** _____ flores

**9.** _____ número

**10.** _____ amigos

**4**

Now look at the next group of possessive adjectives:

|  I | II |
|---|---|
| **Yo tengo *su* libro.** | **Yo tengo *sus* libros.** |
| **Yo veo *su* pluma.** | **Yo veo *sus* plumas.** |

When do you use **su?** _____

When do you use **sus?** _____

Note that both **su** and **sus** have four different meanings.

**su libro** $\begin{cases} your\ book\ (formal) \\ his\ book \\ her\ book \\ their\ book \end{cases}$ **sus plumas** $\begin{cases} your\ pens\ (formal) \\ his\ pens \\ her\ pens \\ their\ pens \end{cases}$

## Actividad F

Fill in the correct possessive adjective, **su** or **sus:**

1. _____ clase

2. _____ perro

3. _____ discos

4. _____ familia

5. _____ profesora

6. _____ dormitorios

7. _____ padres

8. _____ lámpara

9. _____ apartamento

10. _____ sillas

## Actividad G

Express in Spanish:

1. his mother _____

2. her mother _____

**3.** his father  _____

**4.** your sons  _____

**5.** your flower  _____

**6.** her secretary  _____

**7.** their cars  _____

**8.** your doctor  _____

**9.** his lamps  _____

**10.** her grandfather  _____


**5** Let's learn more about possessive adjectives:

|                   I                   |                  II                   |
| :-----------------------------------: | :-----------------------------------: |
| Es *nuestro* gato.                    | Son *nuestros* gatos.                 |
| Es *nuestra* casa.                    | Son *nuestras* casas.                 |

Which subject pronouns do **nuestro, nuestros, nuestra, nuestras**

bring to mind? _____

What do **nuestro, nuestros, nuestra, nuestras** mean?_____

When do you use **nuestro?** _____

**nuestros?** _____

**nuestra?** _____

**nuestras?** _____

## Actividad H

Fill in the correct possessive adjective, **nuestro, nuestros, nuestra, nuestras:**

1. _____ clase

2. _____ perros

3. _____ familia

4. _____ profesor

5. _____ frutas

6. _____ discos

7. _____ abuela

8. _____ comedor

9. _____ sofás

10. _____ secretarias

**6** Let's summarize all the possessive adjectives:

| | |
|---|---|
| **mi, mis** | *my* |
| **tu, tus** | *your* (familiar) |
| **nuestro, nuestra, nuestros, nuestras** | *our* |
| **su, sus** | *your* (formal)<br>*his, her*<br>*your* (plural)<br>*their* |

## Actividad I

Choose the correct possessive adjective:

1. (mi, mis) _____ libros

2. (tu, tus) _____ casa

3. (nuestro, nuestra, nuestros, nuestras) _____ amigos

4. (su, sus) _____ padres

**5.** (su, sus) _____ hermanas

**6.** (mi, mis) _____ lección

**7.** (su, sus) _____ gato

**8.** (su, sus) _____ profesora

**9.** (nuestro, nuestra, nuestros, nuestras) _____ dinero

**10.** (tu, tus) _____ flores

## Actividad J
Express in Spanish:

**1.** our schools _____

**2.** your (*fam.*) newspaper _____

**3.** my car _____

**4.** their teachers _____

**5.** your (*formal*) doctor _____

**6.** our city _____

**7.** her girl friends _____

**8.** my money _____

**9.** your (*fam.*) records _____

**10.** our living room _____

**7** Read this letter that a boy writes home to his parents:

Muy queridos padres,

¡Mi campamento es estupendo! Mis amigos son Juan, Felipe y Andrés. Jugamos al fútbol, nuestro deporte favorito. Nuestros partidos son excelentes. Juan juega muy bien porque practica el deporte con su padre. ¡ Su madre y sus hermanas también juegan al fútbol!

Nuestros consejeros son Roberto y Diego. Ellos tienen la responsabilidad de ayudar a los muchachos y de jugar con nosotros. Sus reglas no son estrictas. Ellos quieren a todos los campistas.

**queridos** *dear*

**el campamento** *the camp*

**el partido** *the match*
**juega** *plays*

**el consejero** *the counselor*
**ayudar** *help*
**reglas** *rules*
**el campista** *the camper*

La comida aquí es horrible. Mamá, sueño con tus hamburguesas, tu ensalada y tus postres. Pero, ¡no te preocupes! Estoy contento.

Gano premios en el campamento. ¿Saben por qué? Porque mi cama y mis cosas están en orden. Uno de mis amigos hace todo por mí.

Su hijo,<br>Rodrigo

**sueño con** *I dream of*
**el postre** *the dessert*
**¡no te preocupes!**
   *don't worry!*

**ganar** *to win*
  **el premio** *the prize*

**hace** *does*

## Actividad K
Complete the sentences:

1. Su campamento es _____.

2. Juan, Felipe y Andrés son _____.

3. Su deporte favorito es _____.

4. Sus partidos son _____.

5. Juan juega muy bien porque practica con _____.

6. _____ y _____ también juegan al fútbol.

7. Roberto y Diego son _____.

8. _____no son estrictas.

9. La comida es _____.

10. Rodrigo gana _____ porque sus cosas están en orden.

# Conversación

## Vocabulario

**¡Ayúdame!** *Help me!*
**se hace tarde** *it's getting late*

**sobre** *on*
**el bolso** *the bag*

# ■ Información personal

Draw your room and label the objects in it.

# Diálogo

Using the picture cues, complete the dialog with the correct Spanish words:

¡Ayúdame!
¿Dónde está mi ⬚ ?            Tu ⬚ está sobre ⬚.

¿Dónde está mi ⬚ ?            Tu ⬚ está sobre ⬚.

¿Dónde están mis ⬚ ?            Tus ⬚ están sobre ⬚.

¿Dónde está mi ⬚ ?            Tienes tu ⬚ en tus ⬚.

# 16 Los números

## Numbers to 100

**1** You are now ready to count to 100. You may want to review first the numbers 1 to 30 in Lesson 6:

| | | | |
|---|---|---|---|
| 40 | **cuarenta** | 50 | **cincuenta** |
| 41 | **cuarenta y uno** | 60 | **sesenta** |
| 42 | **cuarenta y dos** | 70 | **setenta** |
| 43 | **cuarenta y tres** | 80 | **ochenta** |
| 44 | **cuarenta y cuatro** | 90 | **noventa** |
| 45 | **cuarenta y cinco** | 100 | { **ciento** |
| 46 | **cuarenta y seis** | | **cien** (before a noun) |
| 47 | **cuarenta y siete** | | |
| 48 | **cuarenta y ocho** | | |
| 49 | **cuarenta y nueve** | | |

As you can see, it's fairly simple to form numbers in Spanish. Memorize the numbers from 10 to 90 by tens, then add the word **y** (*and*) plus the number from 1 to 9; for example:

| | |
|---|---|
| 51 | **cincuenta y uno** |
| 62 | **sesenta y dos** |
| 73 | **setenta y tres** |
| 85 | **ochenta y cinco** |
| 96 | **noventa y seis** |

## Actividad A

Read the following numbers aloud and place the correct numeral in the space provided:

1. veinte y tres _____    7. doce _____

2. cuarenta y siete _____    8. sesenta y dos _____

3. treinta y uno _____    9. quince _____

4. diez y seis _____    10. trece _____

5. catorce _____    11. once _____

6. cincuenta y nueve _____    12. siete _____

## Actividad B

Match the list of Spanish numbers with the numerals. Write the matching numeral in the space provided:

1. ochenta _____                              61

2. cuarenta y tres _____                      57

3. setenta y uno _____                        24

4. veinte y cuatro _____                      35

5. cincuenta y siete _____                    80

6. sesenta y uno _____                        16

7. treinta y cinco _____                      43

8. ochenta y cuatro _____                     90

9. diez y seis _____                          71

10. noventa _____                             84

## Actividad C

Your teacher will say a number in Spanish. Write down the numeral:

Example: You hear: **diez**    You write: **10**

1. _____      5. _____      8. _____

2. _____      6. _____      9. _____

3. _____      7. _____      10. _____

4. _____

## Actividad D

**¿Qué mira Pedro?** Connect the dots from zero to one hundred to create the picture that will tell you what Pedro is looking at:

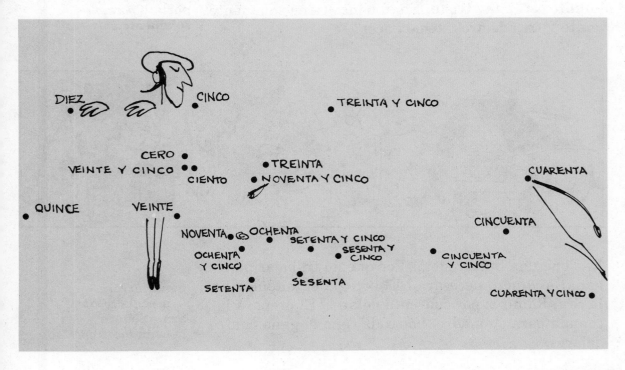

**2** Here is a story about a very ambitious boy. Read it and then do the exercises about it:

La madre de Jaimito odia la música ruidosa.
Entonces Jaimito decide comprar una grabadora
portátil. Pero tiene un problema. El precio de la
grabadora es ciento cincuenta y nueve dólares.
Jaimito está muy triste. En el banco tiene solamente
veinte y tres dólares. ¿Qué hacer?

**odiar** *to hate*
  **ruidoso** *noisy*
**entonces** *so*
  **una grabadora** *a cassette player*
**portátil** *portable*
**solamente** *only*

Él tiene una buena idea. ¿Por qué no trabajar para
ganar el dinero necesario? Él arregla el automóvil de
la Sra. Ramírez por cuarenta dólares. Él prepara la
comida para su madre. Por cada cena él gana cuatro
dólares.

**ganar** *to earn*
  **arregla** *repairs*
**Sra.=Señora**
**la cena** *the dinner*

¡Él prepara catorce cenas! Él cuida a los cuatro niños de los González por tres dólares la hora. Él cuida a los niños durante doce horas. Él pasea el perro del Sr. Santiago por quince dólares.

**cuidar** *to watch*

**durante** *during, for*
  **pasea** *walks*
**Sr.=Señor**

Él suma el dinero. Él llega a la tienda. Compra la grabadora portátil. Jaimito está muy contento. Tiene su grabadora y tiene todavía dinero en el banco.

**sumar** *to add (up)*
  **la tienda** *the store*

**todavía** *still*

## Actividad E
¿Cómo gana Jaimito el dinero?

1. _____

_____

2. _____

_____

3. _____

_____

4. _____

_____

## Actividad F

Complete the chart that Jaimito made to keep track of his money (write out all the numbers in the second column and in the box):

|  | EL DINERO |  | EL TOTAL |
|---|---|---|---|
| El banco | veinte y tres | dólares | $23 |
| La Sra. Ramírez | _____ | dólares | _____ |
| La madre | _____ × _____ = _____ | dólares | _____ |
| Los González | _____ × _____ = _____ | dólares | _____ |
| El Sr. Santiago | _____ | dólares | _____ |

El dinero de Jaimito: _____

La grabadora: _____

Jaimito tiene todavía: _____

## Actividad G

Arithmetic in Spanish. Can you solve these problems?

**1.** Add:

| diez | treinta | setenta |
|---|---|---|
| + cuarenta | + cincuenta | + diez |
| _____ | _____ | _____ |

**2.** Subtract:

| diez y seis | veinte | cincuenta |
|---|---|---|
| − tres | − catorce | − cuarenta |
| _____ | _____ | _____ |

**3.** Multiply:

| tres | diez | dos |
| × nueve | × tres | × siete |

_____  _____  _____

**4.** Divide:

| sesenta | veinte y cuatro | treinta y cinco |
| ÷ tres | ÷ dos | ÷ cinco |

_____  _____  _____

## Actividad H

Rearrange the following list of numbers so that they are in order, the smallest first, the largest last:

**1.** noventa y cinco  _____

**2.** trece  _____

**3.** sesenta  _____

**4.** quince  _____

**5.** cuarenta  _____

**6.** veinte y nueve  _____

**7.** treinta  _____

**8.** setenta y dos  _____

**9.** catorce  _____

**10.** cincuenta  _____

# Actividad I

Write out these numbers in Spanish:

1. 12 _____

2. 49 _____

3. 78 _____

4. 80 _____

5. 19 _____

6. 63 _____

7. 14 _____

8. 36 _____

9. 24 _____

10. 87 _____

11. 51 _____

12. 93 _____

13. 15 _____

14. 76 _____

15. 99 _____

# Conversación

## Vocabulario

**¿Qué haces?** *What are you doing?*
**cuento** *I'm counting*
**hasta** *until*

**el fin** *the end*
**el año escolar** *the school year*
**queremos ayudarte** *we want to help you*

# Diálogo

Choose the question that the second person would ask:

Setenta y uno, setenta y dos, setenta y tres...

¿Qué cantas?
¿Qué haces?
¿Qué usas?

Cuento...
ochenta y uno,
ochenta y dos,
ochenta y tres...

¿Qué cuentas?
¿Qué preparas?
¿Qué contestas?

Cuento la horas,
noventa y uno,
noventa y dos,
noventa y tres...

¿Qué minutos cuentas?
¿Qué horas cuentas?
¿Qué días cuentas?

Cuento las horas
hasta mi fiesta
de sorpresa.

Quiero responderte.
Quiero ayudarte.
Quiero escucharte.

# ■ Información personal

1. Write out four different math problems in Spanish:

   a. _____ + _____ = _____

   b. _____ − _____ = _____

   c. _____ × _____ = _____

   d. _____ ÷ _____ = _____

2. Write out the numbers in Spanish:

   a. The age of your oldest relative _____

   b. The grade on your last Spanish test _____

   c. The number of students in your Spanish class _____

   d. The number of books you have in your room _____

# Repaso IV
# (Lecciones 13–16)

**a.** The verb **tener** is an irregular verb meaning *to have*. Memorize all of its forms:

|       |        |                      |          |
|-------|--------|----------------------|----------|
| yo    | tengo  | nosotros \ nosotras  | tenemos  |
| tú    | tienes |                      |          |

| Ud. \ él \ ella | tiene | Uds. \ ellos \ ellas | tienen |

**b.** Learn the meanings of these special expressions with **tener**. They may be used with any subject representing a person as long as **tener** is conjugated:

| | |
|---|---|
| **tener calor** | *to be warm* |
| **tener frío** | *to be cold* |
| **tener hambre** | *to be hungry* |
| **tener sed** | *to be thirsty* |
| **tener razón** | *to be right* |
| **no tener razón** | *to be wrong* |
| **tener sueño** | *to be sleepy* |
| **tener ___ años** | *to be ___ old* |

Examples: **Yo *tengo* calor.**   *I'm warm.*
**Nosotros *tenemos* sed.**   *We are thirsty.*

If the subject is not a person, use the verb **estar**:

**La comida *está* fría.**   *The food is cold.*

## Lección 14

| LOS DÍAS | LOS MESES | LAS ESTACIONES |
|----------|-----------|----------------|
| el lunes | enero | el invierno |
| el martes | febrero | |
| el miércoles | marzo | |
| el jueves | abril | la primavera |
| el viernes | mayo | |
| el sábado | junio | |
| el domingo | julio | el verano |
| | agosto | |
| | septiembre | |
| | octubre | el otoño |
| | noviembre | |
| | diciembre | |

## Lección 15

The possessive adjectives are used to express that something belongs to someone:

| | |
|---|---|
| **mi, mis** | *my* |
| **tu, tus** | *your* (familiar) |
| **nuestro, nuestra, nuestros, nuestras** | *our* |
| **su, sus** | *your* (formal)<br>*his, her*<br>*your* (plural)<br>*their* |

## Lección 16

| | | | |
|---|---|---|---|
| 40 | cuarenta | 50 | cincuenta |
| 41 | cuarenta y uno | 60 | sesenta |
| 42 | cuarenta y dos | 70 | setenta |
| 43 | cuarenta y tres | 80 | ochenta |
| 44 | cuarenta y cuatro | 90 | noventa |
| 45 | cuarenta y cinco | 100 | ciento<br>cien (before a noun) |
| 46 | cuarenta y seis | | |
| 47 | cuarenta y siete | | |
| 48 | cuarenta y ocho | | |
| 49 | cuarenta y nueve | | |

## Actividad A

After filling in all the letters, look at the vertical box to find the
answer to question **¿Qué te pasa?**:

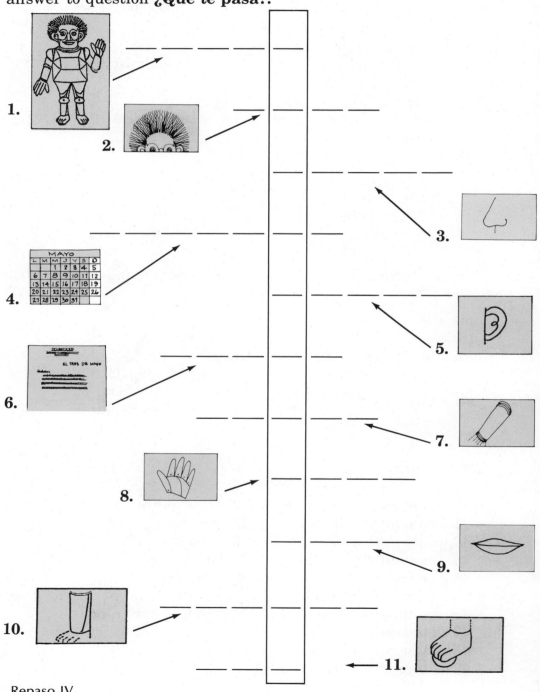

## Actividad B

Use the secret numbers to break the code. The numbers tell you
which letters to put into the boxes:

| CODE | | | | | |
|---|---|---|---|---|---|
| A<br>1 | B<br>2 | C<br>3 | CH<br>4 | D<br>5 | E<br>6 |
| F<br>7 | G<br>8 | H<br>9 | I<br>10 | J<br>11 | K<br>12 |
| L<br>13 | LL<br>14 | M<br>15 | N<br>16 | Ñ<br>17 | O<br>18 |
| P<br>19 | Q<br>20 | R<br>21 | RR<br>22 | S<br>23 | T<br>24 |
| U<br>25 | V<br>26 | W<br>27 | X<br>28 | Y<br>29 | Z<br>30 |

A word that makes the world go round:

| | | | |
|---|---|---|---|
| 1 | 15 | 18 | 21 |

Something you can't seem to have enough of:

| | | | | | |
|---|---|---|---|---|---|
| 5 | 10 | 16 | 6 | 21 | 18 |

We wait for them all year long:

| | | | | | | | | | |
|---|---|---|---|---|---|---|---|---|---|
| 26 | 1 | 3 | 1 | 3 | 10 | 18 | 16 | 6 | 23 |

One of the most important persons in your life:

| | | | | | | | | |
|---|---|---|---|---|---|---|---|---|
| 19 | 21 | 18 | 7 | 6 | 23 | 18 | 21 | 1 |

What many of us would like to be:

| | | | | | | | | | |
|---|---|---|---|---|---|---|---|---|---|
| 15 | 10 | 14 | 18 | 16 | 1 | 21 | 10 | 18 | 23 |

## Actividad C

Each person has a problem. What is it?

1. _____

2. _____

3. _____

5. _____

4. _____

6. _____

## Actividad D

Crucigrama:

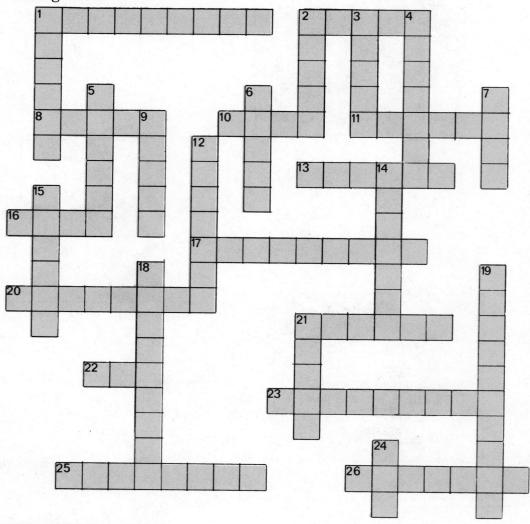

HORIZONTALES

1. Wednesday
2. July
8. January
10. May
11. Saturday
13. Thursday
16. But

17. November
20. Winter
21. August
22. Day
23. December
25. Season
26. February

VERTICALES

1. Tuesday
2. June
3. Monday
4. October
5. Summer
6. March
7. Hour
9. Autumn

12. Sunday
14. Friday
15. Week
18. Spring
19. September
21. April
24. Month

# Actividad E
¿Cuál es la fecha?

1. _____

_____

3. _____

_____

2. _____

_____

4. _____

_____

## Actividad F

Identify the pictures using possessive adjectives:

1. _____

2. _____

3. _____

4. _____

**5.** _____

**7.** _____

**6.** _____

**8.** _____

**9.** _____

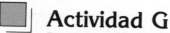

# Actividad G

In this puzzle, you will find 12 parts of the body and 8 items seen around the house. Circle the words from left to right, right to left, up or down, or diagonally:

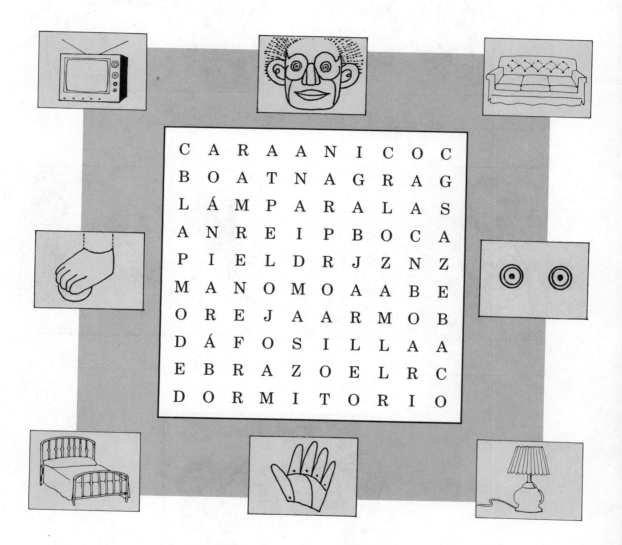

```
C A R A A N I C O C
B O A T N A G R A G
L Á M P A R A L A S
A N R E I P B O C A
P I E L D R J Z N Z
M A N O M O A A B E
O R E J A A R M O B
D Á F O S I L L A A
E B R A Z O E L R C
D O R M I T O R I O
```

## Actividad H

Picture Story. Can you read this story? Much of it is in picture form. Whenever you come to a picture, read it as if it were a Spanish word:

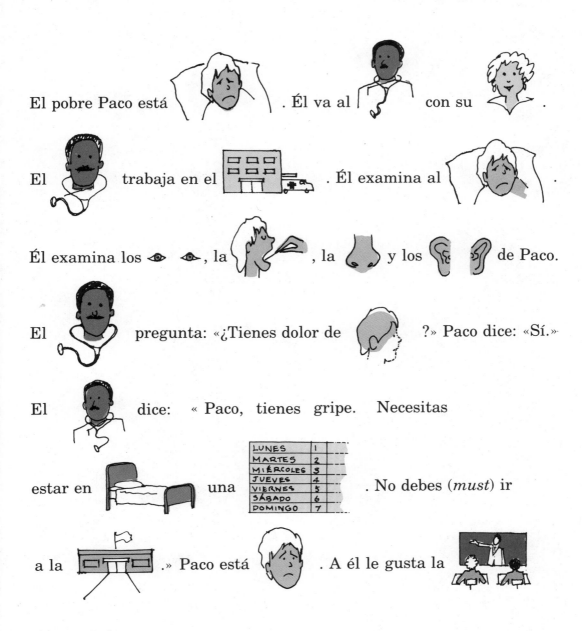

El pobre Paco está [cama] . Él va al [médico] con su [madre] .

El [médico] trabaja en el [hospital] . Él examina al [enfermo] .

Él examina los [ojos] , la [boca] , la [nariz] y los [oídos] de Paco.

El [médico] pregunta: «¿Tienes dolor de [cabeza] ?» Paco dice: «Sí.»

El [médico] dice: « Paco, tienes gripe. Necesitas estar en [cama] una [semana] . No debes (must) ir a la [escuela] .» Paco está [triste] . A él le gusta la [clase] de español.

# Quinta
### Parte

# 17 Los alimentos

What to Say When You Like Something;
the Verbs **gustar** and **querer**

**1** You should like learning this new vocabulary:

**el pan**

**el queso**

**el helado**

**el agua**

**el jugo de naranja**

**el pescado**

**el pollo**

**las legumbres**

**la leche**

**las frutas**

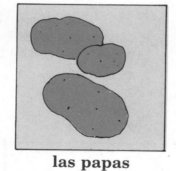

**la carne**

**la sopa**

**las papas**

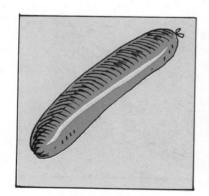

**la salchicha**

**los sandwiches**

**la ensalada**

And you can buy all these things here:

**el supermercado**

 ## Actividad A

Match the words with the pictures:

la carne         la leche
la ensalada      el pan
el helado        el pescado
el jugo de naranja   el queso

1. _____   2. _____   3. _____

**4.** _____

**6.** _____

**7.** _____

**5.** _____

**8.** _____

![icon] **Actividad B**

¿Qué es esto? (*What's that?*)

**1.** _____

**2.** _____

**3.** _____

**4.** _____

**6.** _____

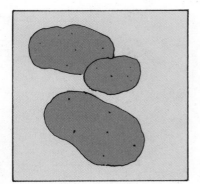

**7.** _____

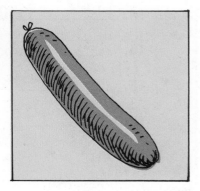

**8.** _____

**5.** _____

 ## Actividad C

Fill in the correct definite article **el, la, los,** or **las:**

1. _____ helado

2. _____ jugo de naranja

3. _____ leche

4. _____ legumbres

5. _____ carne

6. _____ sandwiches

7. _____ queso

8. _____ pescado

9. _____ agua

10. _____ salchicha

11. _____ ensalada

12. _____ pan

13. _____ papas

14. _____ pollo

15. _____ frutas

16. _____ sopa

**2**  Look carefully at these sentences using forms of the verb **gustar** (*to like*):

I                  II

*Me gusta* la leche.    *Me gustan* las frutas.
*Me gusta* el pollo.    *Me gustan* las legumbres.

How many are referred to in each example in Group I? _____

How many are referred to in the examples in Group II? _____

What do both **me gusta** and **me gustan** mean? _____

If you wrote "I like," you are correct. This is how it works:

**Me gusta** is followed by a noun in the SINGULAR:

**Me gusta el libro.**    *I like the book.*

**Me gustan** is followed by a noun in the PLURAL:

**Me gustan los libros.**   *I like the books.*

Let's put it another way: If what is liked is SINGULAR, use **gusta.** If what is liked is PLURAL, use **gustan.**

## Actividad D

Complete the sentences with the correct form of **gustar:**

1. Me _____ la carne.

2. Me _____ las salchichas.

3. Me _____ los jugos.

4. Me _____ el trabajo.

5. Me _____ la televisión.

6. Me _____ las papas.

**3**  Look at these sentences:

| | |
|---|---|
| **Me gusta comer.** | *I like to eat.* |
| **Me gusta bailar.** | *I like to dance.* |
| **Me gusta estudiar.** | *I like to study.* |

**Me gusta** may also be followed by the INFINITIVE of a verb.

**4**

Now that you know how to say *I like* (**me gusta** or **me gustan**), here are the other forms of *to like* in Spanish:

SINGULAR

| | |
|---|---|
| *Te gusta* la bicicleta. | *You* (familiar) *like the bicycle.* |
| *Le gusta* la bicicleta. | {*You* (formal) *like the bicycle.*<br>*He/She likes the bicycle.* |
| *Nos gusta* la bicicleta. | *We like the bicycle.* |
| *Les gusta* la bicicleta. | {*You* (plural) *like the bicycle.*<br>*They like the bicycle.* |

PLURAL

| | |
|---|---|
| *Te gustan* las bicicletas. | *You* (familiar) *like the bicycles.* |
| *Le gustan* las bicicletas. | {*You* (formal) *like the bicycles.*<br>*He/She likes the bicycles.* |
| *Nos gustan* las bicicletas. | *We like the bicycles.* |
| *Les gustan* las bicicletas. | {*You* (plural) *like the bicycles.*<br>*They like the bicycles.* |

Notice that you follow the same rule for all forms: Use **gusta** for the SINGULAR or an INFINITIVE; use **gustan** for the PLURAL. CAUTION: With **gustar,** never use the subject pronouns **yo, tú, él, ella, Ud., nosotros, Uds., ellos, ellas.**

**5**

What happens when you don't like or when someone doesn't like something? Simply place the word **no** before the pronoun:

| | |
|---|---|
| *No* me gusta la leche. | *I don't like (the) milk.* |
| *No* le gustan las legumbres. | *He/She doesn't (You don't) like vegetables.* |

Asking a question is even simpler. Just use a rising pitch of voice when speaking or place question marks when writing:

| | |
|---|---|
| ¿**Te gusta la música?** | *Do you like (the) music?* |
| ¿**No les gustan los discos?** | *Don't you like the records?* |

## Actividad E

Using the pictures as clues, state that the people indicated like what the pictures show. Follow the first example:

**1.** (*I*) Me gusta la profesora.

**2.** (*She*) _____

**3.** (*We*) _____

**4.** (*You, formal*) _____

**5.** (*They*) _____

**6.** (*You, fam.*) _____

**7.** (*He*) _____

**8.** (*You, plural*) _____

**9.** (*They*) _____

**10.** (*You, formal*) _____

## Actividad F
Make all the sentences in Actividad E negative:

**1.** _____

**2.** _____

**3.** _____

**4.** _____

**5.** _____

**6.** _____

**7.** _____

**8.** _____

**9.** _____

**10.** _____

**6** Now look at one more situation involving the use of **gustar:**

> A *Roberto* **le gusta la clase.**
> A *los alumnos* **les gustan las clases.**

Who is doing the liking in the first example? _____

Who is doing the liking in the second example? _____

What little word did we put before **Roberto** and **los alumnos**? _____
It's very simple: To say that someone likes something and the someone is a name or a noun, put **a** plus the name or noun before **le gusta**
or **le gustan**. (Remember that **a + el = al**.)

## Actividad G

Match the English meanings below with the Spanish expressions and
write the matching letters in the spaces provided:

**1.** A mi hermano le gusta estudiar. _____

**2.** A nuestros abuelos les gusta el verano. _____

**3.** Al perro no le gustan los gatos. _____

**4.** ¿A tus padres les gusta el café? _____

**5.** A los alumnos les gustan las vacaciones. _____

**6.** Al padre no le gusta la música ruidosa. _____

**7.** A la señorita le gustan las blusas. _____

**8.** A nuestra profesora le gustan los ejercicios. _____

**a.** The students like the vacation.       **f.** Our teacher likes the exercises.
**b.** The young woman likes the blouses.     **g.** Our grandparents like the summer.
**c.** Do your parents like coffee?           **h.** My sister likes to talk.
**d.** The parents don't like the winter.     **i.** The father doesn't like loud music.
**e.** The dog doesn't like cats.             **j.** My brother likes to study.

**7** Before we read a conversation taking place in an unusual restaurant, there is one more important verb to learn. See if you can understand the following sentences using forms of **querer** (*to want*):

Yo *quiero* una fruta.

Tu *quieres* un pan.
Ud. *quiere* leer.
Él *quiere* queso.

Ella *quiere* un vaso de leche.

Nosotros *queremos* helado de chocolate.

Uds. *quieren* arroz.

Ellos *quieren* una docena de huevos.

Ellas *quieren* aprender.

As you can see, **querer** is somewhat irregular. The endings are regular, but an **i** is inserted in all forms except for **nosotros**:

| | |
|---|---|
| yo **quiero** | *I want* |
| tú **quieres** | *you want* (familiar) |
| Ud. **quiere** | *you want* (formal) |
| él **quiere** | *he wants* |
| ella **quiere** | *she wants* |
| nosotros ⎫<br>nosotras ⎭ **queremos** | *we want* |
| Uds. **quieren** | *you want* (plural) |
| ellos ⎫<br>ellas ⎭ **quieren** | *they want* |

## Actividad H

Complete each sentence with a form of the verb **querer** and the name of the object shown in the picture:

1. Tú _____ una _____.

**2.** Ella _____ _____.

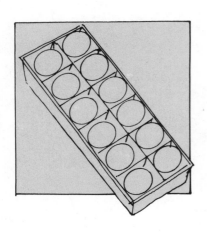

**3.** Uds. _____ una _____ de _____.

**4.** Él _____ un _____.

**5.** Nosotros _____ _____.

**6.** María _____ un _____.

**7.** Ellos _____ un _____ de _____.

**8.** Yo _____ mucho _____ .

**8** Now enjoy this conversation in a very special restaurant:

| | | |
|---|---|---|
| EL CAMARERO: | Muy buenas tardes. ¿Qué desean Uds.? | **el camarero** *the waiter* |
| LA SEÑORA: | Para mí, una ensalada mixta de lechuga y tomate con huevos duros y una soda. Me gustan la lechuga y los tomates. | **mixta** *mixed* <br> **la lechuga** *the lettuce* <br> **huevos duros** *hard-boiled eggs* |
| EL CAMARERO: | Muy bien. ¿Y Ud., señor? | |
| EL SEÑOR: | Bueno, el arroz con pollo y un vaso de jugo de naranja. | **el arroz** *the rice* <br> **el vaso** *the glass* |
| EL CAMARERO: | Lo siento, señor, pero no tenemos arroz con pollo. | **lo siento** *I'm sorry* |

| EL SEÑOR: | Entonces, una hamburguesa con queso y papas fritas. | **papas fritas** *french fries* |
| EL CAMARERO: | No hay hamburguesa, señor. | |

| EL SEÑOR: | En ese caso, quiero un bistec con puré de papas. | **el bistec** *the steak* |
| | | **el puré de papas** *mashed potatoes* |
| EL CAMARERO: | Lo siento otra vez, pero no tenemos bistec. | **otra vez** *again* |
| EL SEÑOR: | ¡Caramba! ¿Qué pasa aquí? Me gusta la carne. ¿Por qué no tienen nada? | **nada** *nothing* |
| LA SEÑORA: | Ay, mi amor. Mira el menú. Es un restaurante vegetariano. | **mi amor** *my love* |

## Actividad I
Complete the sentences:

**1.** La señora quiere _____.

**2.** El señor quiere _____

_____.

**3.** También _____ tomar un vaso de _____.

**4.** El restaurante no tiene _____.

**5.** Es un restaurante _____.

# Conversación

**Vocabulario**

el pastel *the cake*

**por favor** *please*

# Preguntas personales

1. Si tienes hambre, ¿qué te gusta comer?

   _____

2. ¿Te gustan las legumbres?

   _____

3. ¿Te gustan las frutas?

   _____

4. ¿Qué no te gusta comer?

   _____

5. ¿Qué postre te gusta?

   _____

# Información personal

¿Qué te gusta comer en el restaurante? Me gusta comer

1. _____

2. _____

3. _____

4. _____

5. _____

# Diálogo

You are the second person in the dialog. Write an original response to each dialog line following the cues provided:

# 18 La ropa; los colores

**1**  Can you guess the meanings of these words?

**la ropa**

**el traje**

**el vestido**

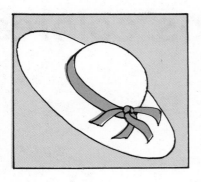

**el sombrero**

**el abrigo**

**el suéter**

**la camisa**

**la blusa**

**la falda**

**la chaqueta**

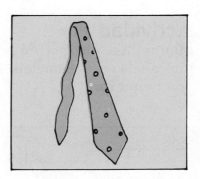

**la corbata**

**los pantalones**

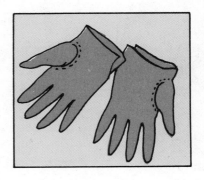

**los guantes**

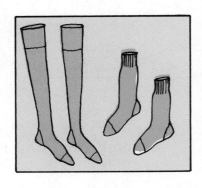

**las medias/los calcetines**

**los zapatos**

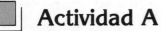

## Actividad A

Manuel has just gotten a job in a clothing store. The boss asks him to pin labels on the models so that the prices can be put on later. Can you help him?

LABELS

| el abrigo | la falda | el sombrero |
|-----------|----------|-------------|
| la blusa | las medias | el suéter |
| la camisa | los pantalones | el vestido |
| la corbata | los guantes | los zapatos |

## Actividad B

Identify the article of clothing:

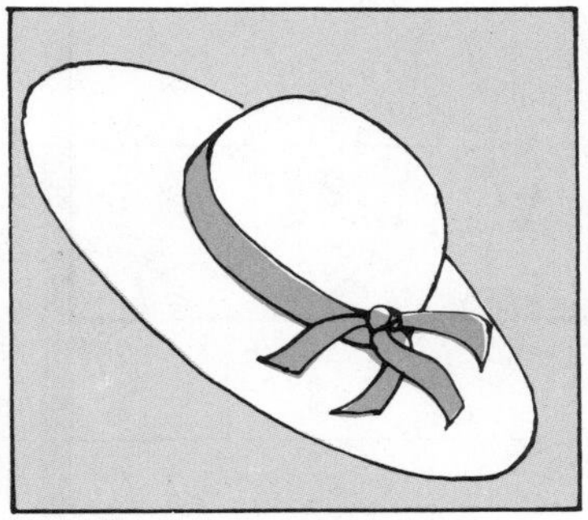

1. ______________________

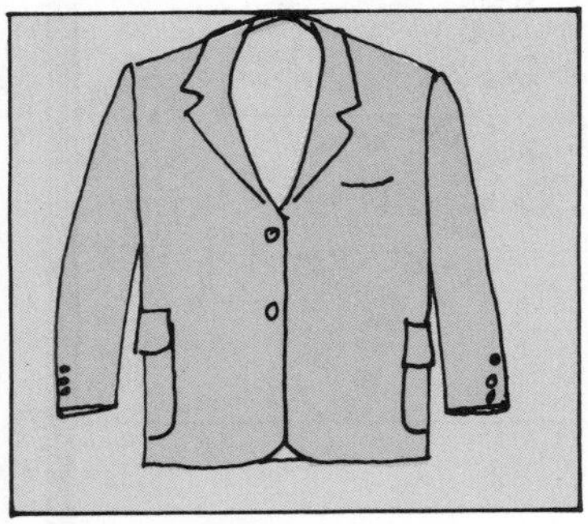

2. ______________________

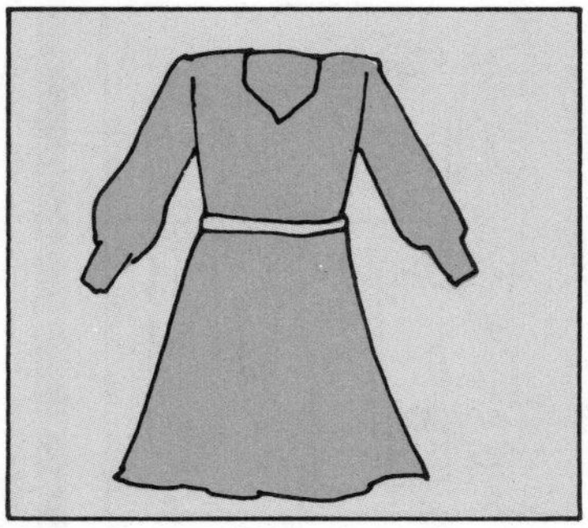

3. ______________________

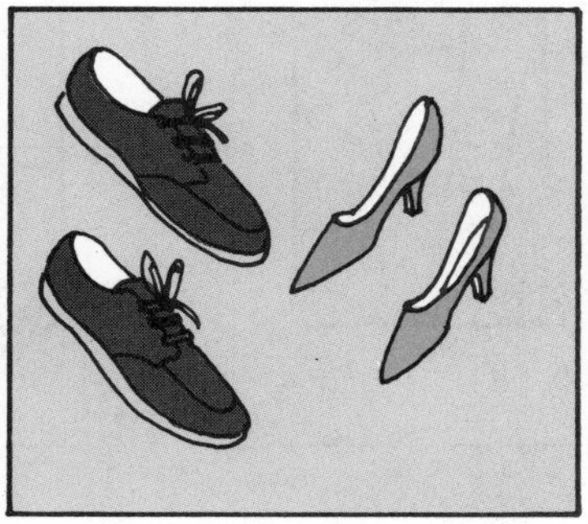

4. ______________________

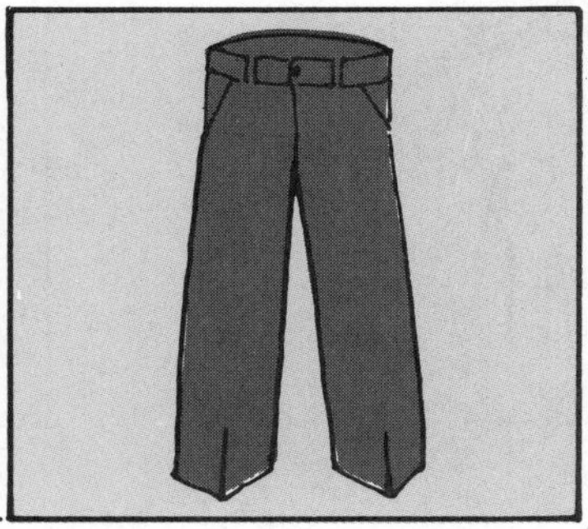

5. ______________________

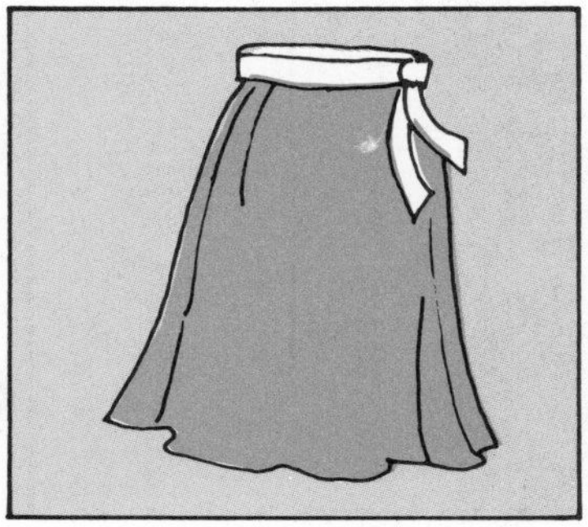

6. ______________________

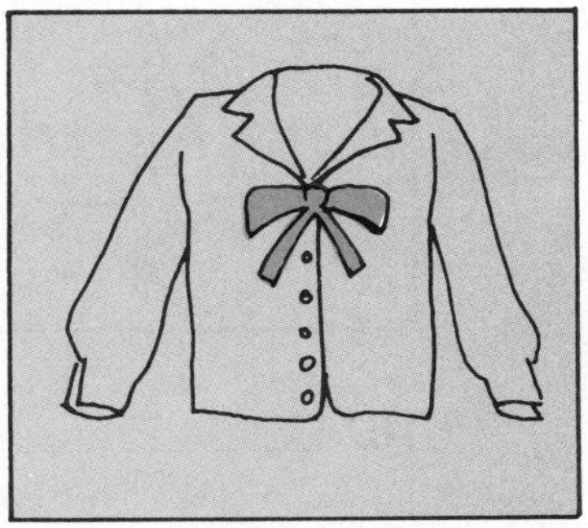

7. ______________________

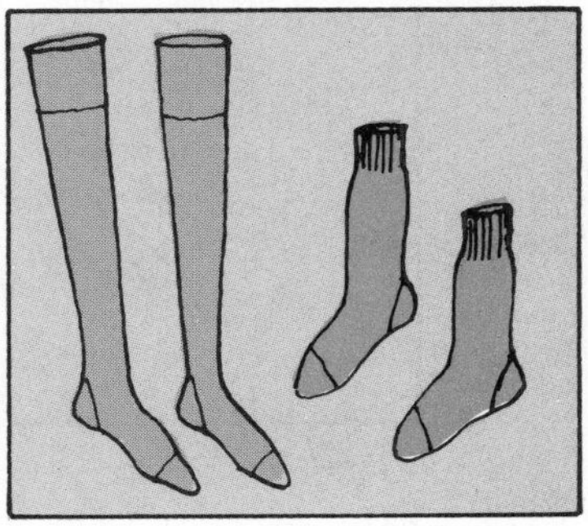

8. ______________________

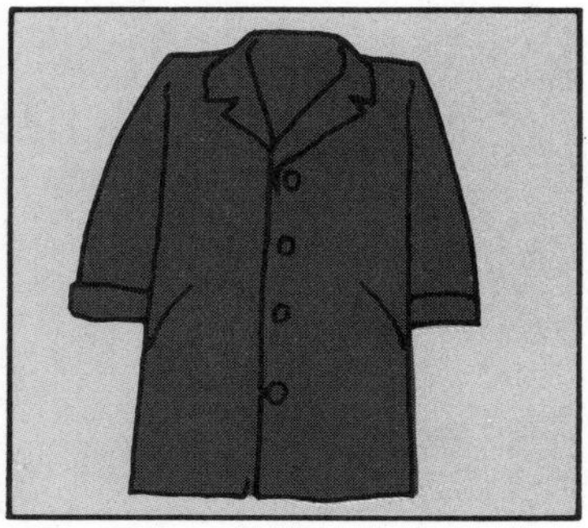

9. ______________________

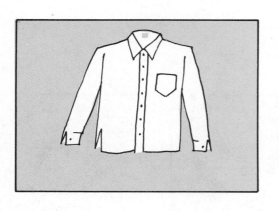

**10.** _____

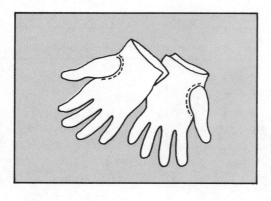

**11.** _____

**12.** _____

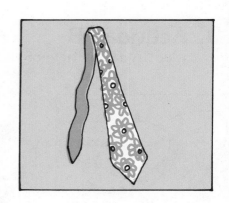

**13.** _____

**14.** _____

**15.** _____

**2**  Learn the names of the colors:

| | |
|---|---|
| **amarillo** *(yellow)* | **negro** *(black)* |
| **anaranjado** *(orange)* | **pardo, castaño** *(brown)* |
| **azul** *(blue)* | **rojo** *(red)* |
| **blanco** *(white)* | **rosado** *(pink)* |
| **gris** *(gray)* | **verde** *(green)* |

Colors are adjectives. As you learned in Lesson 8, adjectives agree in gender and number with the nouns they describe. Adjectives of color follow the same rules, and they also come after the noun. Here are some examples:

| MASCULINE SINGULAR | FEMININE SINGULAR |
|---|---|
| **el automóvil roj*o*** | **la casa roj*a*** |
| **el libro amarill*o*** | **la pluma amarill*a*** |

But:

| | |
|---|---|
| **el lápiz verd*e*** | **la mesa verd*e*** |
| **el papel azul** | **la silla azul** |

| MASCULINE PLURAL | FEMININE PLURAL |
|---|---|
| **los libros roj*os*** | **las casas roj*as*** |
| **los papeles azul*es*** | **las sillas azul*es*** |

## Actividad C

Identify the object and the color. Use the correct definite article. Follow the example:

**1. el sombrero blanco**

2. _____
  (red)

**3.** _____
(yellow)

**6.** _____
(blue)

**4.** _____
(black)

**7.** _____
(brown)

**5.** _____
(orange)

**8.** _____
(green)

## Actividad D

Describe what you see. Follow the example:

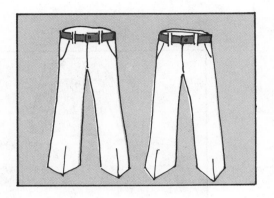

**1. pantalones rojos**

3. _____
   (gray)

2. _____
   (white)

4. _____
   (yellow)

La ropa; los colores    **343**

**5.** _____
(black)

**7.** _____
(pink)

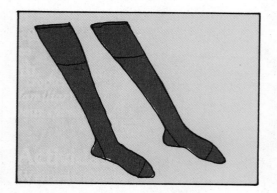

**6.** _____
(blue)

**8.** _____
(brown)

**3**  Now read this story and then do the exercise that follows:

El profesor de español, el señor Romero, es un profesor excelente, con mucha imaginación. Los alumnos adoran al señor Romero porque sus lecciones son siempre divertidas.

**divertido** *amusing*

Un día, el señor Romero da una lección sobre la ropa y los colores. Da un ejercicio interesante a la clase para practicar el vocabulario. Propone un concurso entre los miembros de la clase. El alumno o la alumna con la ropa más original gana el premio (un disco de música española). Después del concurso, los alumnos hablan de la ropa diferente y así practican el español.

**da** *gives*

**propone** *he proposes*
**el concurso** *the contest*

¡Qué concurso tan bueno! Los alumnos preparan ropa extraordinaria. Roberto lleva un sombrero amarillo, un suéter anaranjado y pantalones verdes. Carmencita lleva una blusa rosada, una falda anaranjada, medias pardas, pero no lleva zapatos. Finalmente, la ropa más original es la ropa de_____. Aquí está su ropa: (Draw and describe the outfit.)

**llevar** *to wear*

**finalmente** *finally*

## Actividad E

**¿Cierto o falso?** If the answer is **falso,** correct the sentence:

1. El señor Romero es el profesor de **biología.** _____

2. Es un profesor con mucha **ropa.** _____

3. Da una lección sobre **la cultura.** _____

4. Da un ejercicio **delicioso.** _____

5. Hay **un concurso.** _____

6. Los alumnos preparan **comida** diferente. _____

7. El premio es **un libro.** _____

8. La ropa diferente es **horrible.** _____

**346**    Lección 18

# Conversación

## Vocabulario

**buscar** *to look for*
**el par** *the pair*

**invitada** *invited*
**la fiesta de disfraces** *the costume party*

# Diálogo

You are the first person in the dialog. Tell the salesman exactly what you are looking for:

# ◻ Información personal

Describe the five articles of clothing that you like best:

Example: Me gusta un traje rojo.

1. _____

2. _____

3. _____

4. _____

5. _____

# 19 ¿Qué tiempo hace?

Weather Expressions; the Verbs **hacer** and **ir**

**1** **¿Qué tiempo hace?**

Es la primavera.
Hace buen tiempo.
Hace viento.

Es el verano.
Hace calor.
Hace sol.

Es el otoño.
Hace mal tiempo.
Hace fresco.
Llueve.

Es el invierno.
Hace frío.
Nieva.

# Actividad A

Match the following expressions with the correct pictures:

**Hace buen tiempo.**    **Hace viento.**
**Hace mal tiempo.**    **Hace sol.**
**Hace frío.**    **Nieva.**
**Hace calor.**    **Llueve.**

1. _____

3. _____

2. _____

4. _____

5. _____

7. _____

6. _____

8. _____

## Actividad B
¿Qué tiempo hace?

1. _____

2. _____

**3.** _____

**6.** _____

**4.** _____

**7.** _____

**5.** _____

**8.** _____

¿Qué tiempo hace?    **353**

**2** In the story that follows, all the forms of the verb **hacer** *(to make, to do)* appear. See if you can find them all?

## COMPOSICIÓN

Yo me llamo: *Luis Ponce*   Clase: *Español*

Fecha: *El seis de enero*   Profesor(a): *Sra. López*

Cuando **hace** frío en el invierno, voy rápidamente a casa. Mamá **hace** chocolate y yo **hago** mis tareas inmediatamente. Cuando nieva, salgo de la casa y juego con mis amigos en la nieve. **Hacemos** una figura de nieve. Mis amigos siempre preguntan: «Luis, ¿tú vas a esquiar con nosotros?» Respondo: «No». Prefiero lanzar bolas de nieve a las muchachas. (La verdad es que no me gusta esquiar.) Entonces ellas **hacen** muecas y gritan: «¡Ay, Luis!, ¿qué **haces**?» Estoy muy contento cuando nieva.

**a casa** *home*

**la figura de nieve** *the snowman*
**tú vas a esquiar** *are you going skiing*
**lanzar** *to throw*
  **la bola de nieve** *the snowball*
**hacer muecas** *to make faces*
  **gritar** *to cry out*

**354**   Lección 19

## Actividad C

Complete the sentences:

1. El alumno se llama _____.

2. La composición habla del _____.

3. Luis va _____ rápidamente.

4. La madre hace _____.

5. Luis sale de la casa cuando _____.

6. Los amigos hacen una _____.

7. Los amigos también van a _____.

8. Luis tiene _____.

9. Él lanza _____ a las muchachas.

10. Ellas hacen _____.

**3** Did you find the forms of the verb **hacer** in the story? **Hacer** has some irregular forms. **Hacer** means *to make, to do*. Fill in the proper forms of **hacer** for each subject. MEMORIZE them:

yo _____

tú _____

Ud. _____

él _____

ella _____

nosotros⎫
nosotras⎭ _____

Uds. _____

ellos _____

ellas _____

**4** Now look carefully at these sentences:

| | |
|---|---|
| **Hace calor.** | **Hace viento.** |
| **Hace frío.** | **Hace buen tiempo.** |
| **Hace sol.** | **Hace mal tiempo.** |

**Hacer** is used to express weather conditions.

## Actividad D

Can you match these sentences with the pictures they describe?

| | |
|---|---|
| **Ellas hacen tortillas.** | **Hacen una figura de nieve.** |
| **Hace calor.** | **Hace buen tiempo.** |
| **Hago mis tareas.** | **¿Por qué haces muecas?** |

1. _____

3. _____

2. _____

4. _____

**5.** _____    **6.** _____

 ## Actividad E
Answer the questions:

**1.** ¿Qué tiempo hace hoy?

_____

**2.** ¿Qué haces cuando hace calor?

_____

**3.** ¿Qué haces en el invierno?

_____

**4.** ¿A qué hora haces tus tareas?

_____

**5.** ¿En qué estación hacen tus amigos y tú bolas de nieve?

_____

**5** Can you guess the meanings of these sentences? All include a form of the important Spanish verb **ir** (*to go*):

**Yo *voy* a casa.**

**Tu *vas* al cine.**

**Él *va* al parque.**

**Ella *va* al teatro.**

**Ud. *va* al banco.**

**Uds. *van* a la tienda.**

**Nosotros *vamos* a la escuela.**

**Ellos *van* a la fiesta.**

**Ellas *van* a la playa.**

The verb **ir** is important and also very irregular. Repeat the forms of **ir** and MEMORIZE them:

| | | |
|---|---|---|
| yo voy | | *I go* |
| tú vas | | *you go* (familiar) |
| Ud. va | | *you go* (formal) |
| él va | | *he goes* |
| ella va | | *she goes* |
| nosotros }<br>nosotras } | vamos | *we go* |
| Uds. van | | *you go* (plural) |
| ellos }<br>ellas } | van | *they go* |

## Actividad F

Fill in the correct form of the verb **ir**:

1. Los muchachos _____ a la escuela.

2. Ellas _____ en el automóvil.

3. Ud. _____ al parque.

4. Él _____ a la fiesta.

5. Yo _____ a San Juan.

6. María _____ a la tienda.

7. Nosotros _____ al hotel.

8. Tú _____ a la playa.

# Información personal

You are the weather forecaster for your school. Give the weather for the following dates:

1. el veinte y uno de septiembre

_____

2. el treinta de enero

_____

3. el veinte y dos de abril

_____

4. el diez y seis de junio

_____

# Conversación

## Vocabulario

**caerme** *fall (down)*
**No importa.** *It doesn't matter.*

**¡Vamos!** *Let's go!*

# Diálogo

You are the first person in the following dialog, the one asking all the questions:

# 20 Los animales

## The Verb **decir**

**1** Can you guess the meanings of these words?

**el gato**

**el perro**

**el caballo**

**la vaca**

**el cochino**

**el león**

**363**

**el mono**

**el tigre**

**el elefante**

**la gallina**

**el pez**

**el pato**

## Actividad A
Identify. Use the correct definite article:

**1.** _____

**4.** _____

**2.** _____

**5.** _____

**3.** _____

**6.** _____

7. _____

9. _____

8. _____

10. _____

 ## Actividad B

List the animals in their proper settings:

_____

_____

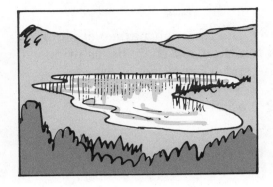

_____

_____

_____

_____

_____

_____

_____

_____

_____

_____

## Actividad C

**¿Quién soy?** Now that you know the Spanish names of some animals, let's see if you can match them by their descriptions. Write the matching letter in the space provided:

1. el perro _____   **a.** Yo galopo.

2. el gato _____   **b.** Yo doy *(give)* la leche.

3. la gallina _____   **c.** Soy el amigo del hombre.

4. el elefante _____   **d.** Me gusta el LODO .

5. el caballo _____   **e.** Soy el de la jungla.

6. el mono _____   **f.** Soy feroz.

7. el tigre _____   **g.** Me gustan los .

8. el cochino _____   **h.** Soy grande y gris.

9. el león _____   **i.** Yo doy los .

10. la vaca _____   **j.** Vivo *(I live)* en los árboles.

## Actividad D

Can you name all the animals on this farm? Start each sentence with **Yo veo:**

1. _____

2. _____

3. _____

4. _____

5. _____

6. _____

## Actividad E

Find the hidden animals. There are 10 animals hidden in this picture. Find them and list them below:

1. _____    6. _____

2. _____    7. _____

3. _____    8. _____

4. _____    9. _____

5. _____    10. _____

**2**   Can you understand this interview with a dog lover?

EL REPÓRTER:  Aquí está la señora Merola con su
famosa perra, Fifí. La perra gana
concursos, recibe muchos premios y
tiene muchas medallas. Si Ud. desea
tener un perro fabuloso, escuche la
entrevista. Señora Merola, ¿cómo
juega su perra?

**la perra** *the (female) dog*

**la entrevista** *the interview*

SRA. MEROLA:  Juega muy bien. Fifí adora a los niños
pequeños porque le dan sus bizcochos.

EL REPÓRTER:  ¿Cuándo da la pata?

**le dan** *give her*
**el bizcocho** *the biscuit*

SRA. MEROLA: Da la pata cuando está contenta.   **la pata** *the paw*
EL REPÓRTER: ¿Qué come?
SRA. MEROLA: Mi cena, naturalmente.
EL REPÓRTER: ¿Por qué es simpática?   **simpática** *nice*
SRA. MEROLA: Porque lo tiene todo.
EL REPÓRTER: ¿Dónde juega?
SRA. MEROLA: Juega en el parque y en mi cama.
EL REPÓRTER: ¿A quién ama?   **ama** *does she love*
SRA. MEROLA: ¡Qué pregunta tan estúpida! Me ama
a mí, por supuesto, porque es mi   **por supuesto** *of course*
nena.   **la nena** *the baby*

## Actividad F

Below are Señora Merola's answers. Can you give the reporter's questions? Be careful. They are not in the same order:

1. _____
   Porque lo tiene todo.

**2.** _____

Da la pata cuando está contenta.

**3.** _____

Juega muy bien.

**4.** _____

Mi cena, naturalmente.

**5.** _____

Juega en el parque.

**6.** _____

Me ama a mí, por supuesto, porque es mi nena.

**3** Here's our final verb — **decir** *(to say, to tell):*

| | |
|---|---|
| **yo digo** | *I say, I tell* |
| **tú dices** | *you say, you tell* (familiar) |
| **Ud. dice** | *you say, you tell* (formal) |
| **él dice** | *he says, he tells* |
| **ella dice** | *she says, she tells* |
| **nosotros** } **decimos**<br>**nosotras** | *we say, we tell* |
| **Uds. dicen** | *you say, you tell* (plural) |
| **ellos** } **dicen**<br>**ellas** | *they say, they tell* |

As you can see, the forms of **decir** do not follow the regular **-ir** verbs that you learned in Lesson 10. The endings are regular, but the **e** in **decir** changes to **i** in all forms except the **nosotros** form (**decimos**).

## Actividad G

Fill in the correct form of **decir**:

1. Yo siempre _____ la verdad (*the truth*).

2. ¿_____ Ud. que él no tiene dinero?

3. ¿Qué _____ tus padres?

4. Nosotros _____ que no queremos ir.

5. ¿Por qué no _____ que no sabes hablar inglés?

## Actividad H

Match the sentences with the correct pictures:

**La radio dice que va a llover mañana.**
**María dice que tenemos mucho tiempo.**
**Digo que hoy es lunes.**
**Dicen que el examen es muy difícil.**
**¿Tú dices que tienes razón?**
**¿Qué decimos a la profesora si no hacemos
    nuestras tareas?**

1. _____

2. _____

3. _____

5. _____

4. _____

6. _____

Los animales   **375**

# Conversación

# Información personal

Draw or find a picture of your favorite animal. Describe the animal in five sentences:

# Diálogo

Rearrange the lines of dialog so that they are in logical order. Number the panels in accordance with the right order:

# Repaso V
# (Lecciones 17–20)

## Lección 17

**a.** Expressing "to like" in Spanish:

|  |  |
|---|---|
| **me gusta(n)** | *I like* |
| **te gusta(n)** | *you like* (familiar) |
| **le gusta(n)** | $\begin{cases} you \text{ like (formal)} \\ he \ likes \\ she \ likes \end{cases}$ |
| **nos gusta(n)** | *we like* |
| **les gusta(n)** | $\begin{cases} you \text{ like (plural)} \\ they \ like \end{cases}$ |

**b.** The verb **querer** *(to want)* has irregular forms. MEMORIZE them:

|  |  |
|---|---|
| **yo quiero** | $\left.\begin{array}{l}\textbf{nosotros}\\\textbf{nosotras}\end{array}\right\}$ **queremos** |
| **tú quieres** |  |
| $\left.\begin{array}{l}\textbf{Ud.}\\\textbf{él}\\\textbf{ella}\end{array}\right\}$ **quiere** | $\left.\begin{array}{l}\textbf{Uds.}\\\textbf{ellos}\\\textbf{ellas}\end{array}\right\}$ **quieren** |

## Lección 18

Colors, like other adjectives, agree in gender and number with the nouns they describe:

| | |
|---|---|
| **el sombrero amarill***o* | **los sombreros amarill***os* |
| **la blusa blan***ca* | **las blusas blan***cas* |
| **el traje azul** | **los trajes azul***es* |
| **la camisa azul** | **las camisas azul***es* |

## Lección 19

**a.** The verb **hacer** is an irregular verb meaning *to make, to do*. MEMORIZE all of its forms:

| | |
|---|---|
| yo hago | nosotros⎫ |
| tú haces | nosotras⎭ hacemos |
| Ud. hace | Uds. hacen |
| él hace | ellos⎫ |
| ella hace | ellas⎭ hacen |

**b.** **Hacer** is used in expressions of weather:

| | |
|---|---|
| **Hace (mucho) calor.** | *It's (very) hot.* |
| **Hace (mucho) frío.** | *It's (very) cold.* |
| **Hace fresco.** | *It's cool.* |
| **Hace (mucho) sol.** | *It's (very) sunny.* |
| **Hace (mucho) viento.** | *It's (very) windy.* |
| **Hace buen tiempo.** | *It's beautiful.* |
| **Hace mal tiempo.** | *It's bad (weather).* |

Note also: **Llueve.** *It's raining*
**Nieva.** *It's snowing*

**c.** The verb **ir** *(to go)* has irregular forms. MEMORIZE them:

| | |
|---|---|
| yo voy | nosotros⎫ |
| tú vas | nosotras⎭ vamos |
| Ud.⎫ | Uds.⎫ |
| él⎬ va | ellos⎬ van |
| ella⎭ | ellas⎭ |

## Lección 20

The verb **decir** *(to say, to tell)* has irregular forms except for the **nosotros** form:

| | |
|---|---|
| yo digo | nosotros⎫ |
| tú dices | nosotras⎭ decimos |
| Ud.⎫ | Uds.⎫ |
| él⎬ dice | ellos⎬ dicen |
| ella⎭ | ellas⎭ |

## Actividad A

Every day, Pedro González and Elena Vegas leave their house and walk to their school, taking the shortest route. On their way they pass many places. Figure out the shortest way to school and list the places they pass:

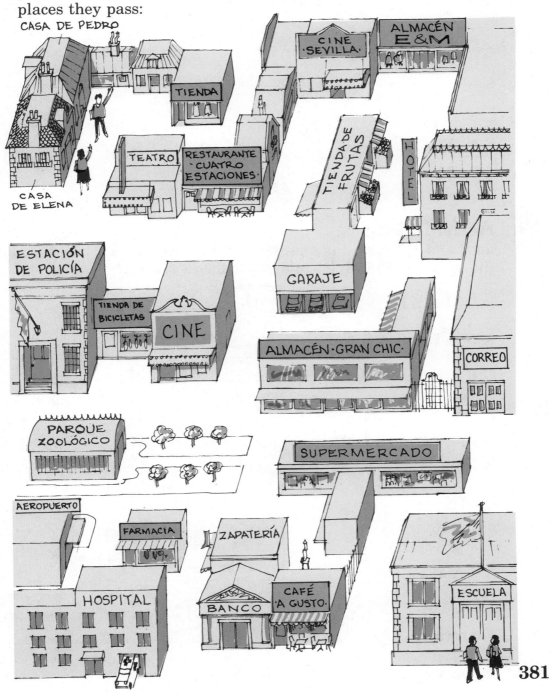

_____

_____

_____

_____

_____

_____

_____

## Actividad B

Food and Clothing Jumbles. Unscramble the words. Then unscramble
the letters in the circles to find out the messages:

D O H A L E  □ Ⓞ Ⓞ □ □ □

A N A L D E A S  □ □ Ⓞ □ Ⓞ □ □ □

G R A S U E M A B U H  □ □ Ⓞ Ⓞ □ □ Ⓞ □ □ □ Ⓞ

R E C R E S O D U M P A  Ⓞ Ⓞ □ Ⓞ □ □ □ Ⓞ □ □ □

**A Juan no le gustan** _____.

D I V O T E S  □ □ □ Ⓞ □ Ⓞ □

S E M I D A  □ Ⓞ □ Ⓞ □ □

A S A M I C  □ Ⓞ □ □ □ Ⓞ

S O L T A N E P N A  □ Ⓞ □ □ □ Ⓞ □ Ⓞ □ □

**Juanita va** _____.

## Actividad C

Crucigrama:

HORIZONTALES

**1.** (we) say
**4.** (we) want
**6.** trousers
**9.** suit
**10.** (they) go
**11.** you
**12.** no
**14.** gray
**15.** pig
**16.** yes
**17.** vegetables
**21.** so
**23.** coat
**24.** fish

VERTICALES

**1.** sports
**2.** movie
**3.** dress
**4.** cheese
**5.** supermarket
**7.** yellow
**8.** shirt
**13.** chicken
**16.** soup
**18.** cat
**19.** monkey
**20.** red
**22.** (he) goes

## Actividad D

Write the Spanish words under the pictures. Then circle the words in the puzzle on page 386. The words may be read from left to right, right to left, up or down, or diagonally:

1. _____

2. _____

3. _____

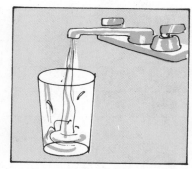

4. _____

5. _____

6. _____

7. _____

8. _____

9. _____

10. _____

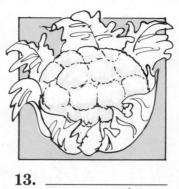

13. _____

17. _____

11. _____

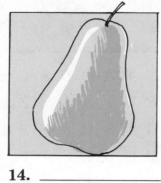

14. _____

18. _____

12. _____

15. _____

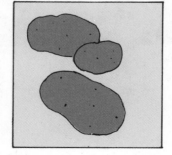

16. _____

19. _____

```
Q S A N T A O D A C S E P
U A F R U T A E H E E O C
E P F G T S R E H B L A A
S A A M O B L C I L R U D
O P O V M A I S O N C N A
U G E U D W T W E H C E L
J U G O D E N A R A N J A
H E O N C H R A P X E T S
L C A F É A P S P O P A N
A S A L C H I C H A S P E
```

## Actividad E

**¿Qué lleva Micaela a la fiesta?** To find out, identify the objects in the pictures. Then write the letters in the blanks, below:

1. _ _ _ _
   1 2

3. _ _ _ _ _
   5 6 7

4. _ _ _ _ _ _ _
   8     9     10

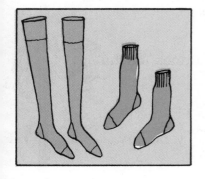

2. _ _ _ _ _ _
   3 4

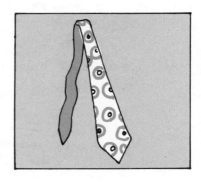

5. _ _ _ _ _ _ _
   11 12

Solution: un _ _ _ _ _ _ _ _  _ _ _ _
          10 11 3 5 1 4 12 2  9 8 7 6

## Actividad F

Picture Stories. Read these stories. Much of them is in picture form. Whenever you come to a picture, read it as if it were a Spanish word:

Todo el mundo habla del [picture]. Siempre preguntan:

¿Qué [picture] hace? En el [picture], hace mucho [picture].

Llevamos un [picture] y [picture]. En la [picture]

y en el [picture] hace [picture] y llevamos una [picture].

En el [picture] hace mucho [picture]. No necesitamos mucha [picture]

Vamos a la [picture]. Hay mucho [picture] y no hay [picture].

¿Cuál es tu estación favorita? ¿Es la [picture], el [picture],

el [picture] o el [picture]?

Hay una  en la de Jorge. Las

y los llegan a la a . Escuchan ,

y . La y el sirven , ,

, , , y . Es el cumpleaños

de Jorge. Desde hoy, el SEPT. 21 , Jorge tiene años.

# Achievement Test II
# (Lessons 13-20)

**1**  Vocabulario [10 points]

1. _____

3. _____

2. _____

4. _____

**5.** _____

**8.** _____

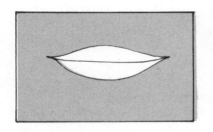

**6.** _____

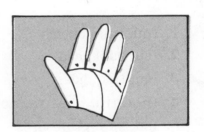

**9.** _____

**7.** _____

**10.** _____

## 2 Numbers [5 points]
You will hear five numbers in Spanish. Write them in numerals:

1. _____

2. _____

3. _____

4. _____

5. _____

## 3 Choose the correct possessive adjectives [5 points]

1. (mi, mis) clases
2. (su, sus) casa
3. (tu, tus) ojos
4. (nuestro, nuestra, nuestros, nuestras) manos
5. (su, sus) profesores

## 4 Dates [5 points]
You will hear 5 dates in Spanish. Write out the date you hear in English:

Example: You hear: **Es el tres de mayo.**
You write: **It's May 3.**

1. _____

2. _____

3. _____

4. _____

5. _____

# 5

Days [5 points]
You will hear the names of 5 days in Spanish. Write the name of the day you hear in English:

Example: You hear: **Es lunes.**
You write: **It's Monday.**

1. _____

2. _____

3. _____

4. _____

5. _____

# 6

Questions [5 points]
You will hear 5 questions. After each question, choose the best suggested answer and write the letter in the space provided:

1. a. Es el diez de junio
   b. Es domingo
   c. Es el verano.

   1. _____

2. a. Estoy en la clase.
   b. Voy a la escuela.
   c. Estoy bien, gracias.

   2. _____

3. a. Hace calor.
   b. Estamos en la primavera.
   c. Hoy es miércoles.

   3. _____

4. a. Son las diez.
   b. Hace fresco.
   c. Hago una visita.

   4. _____

5. a. Tengo catorce años.
   b. Tengo gripe.
   c. Tengo una hermana.

   5. _____

# 7

**¿Qué tiempo hace?** Expressions of weather [6 points]

1. _____

4. _____

2. _____

5. _____

3. _____

6. _____

**394** Achievement Test II

**8** **¿Qué estación es?** The seasons [4 points]

1. _____

3. _____

2. _____

4. _____

**9** Verbs [30 points]

**tener**

1. Yo _____ dos hermanos.

2. Nosotros _____ un buen profesor.

3. Tú _____ razón.

4. Ud. _____ el disco.

5. Ella _____ hambre.

6. Uds. _____ quince años.

**hacer**

7. _____ frío.

8. ¿Qué _____ tú?

9. Yo _____ mis tareas.

10. Ellas _____ una figura de nieve.

11. Ud. _____ chocolate.

12. Nosotros _____ muecas.

**gustar**

13. Le _____ el teatro.

14. ¿No te _____ el helado?

15. Nos _____ los discos.

16. Me _____ la primavera.

17. No le _____ las legumbres.

18. ¿Te _____ la música moderna?

**ir**

19. María y Pablo _____ al cine.

20. Yo _____ a la escuela a las ocho.

**21.** Nosotros _____ a la fiesta.

**22.** ¿_____ Ud. con sus amigos?

**23.** ¡Tú no _____ al parque!

**24.** Ellas _____ siempre a la playa.

**decir**

**25.** Él _____ siempre la verdad.

**26.** ¿Qué _____ yo a la profesora?

**27.** Nosotros _____ que mañana es domingo.

**28.** ¿Qué _____ Uds. a sus padres?

**29.** Ellas _____ que su casa es grande.

**30.** ¿Cuándo _____ tú «Lo siento»?

# 10 Colors [10 points]

Write the correct form of the Spanish color:

**1.** (white)  el papel _____

**2.** (red)  los zapatos _____

**3.** (black)  la corbata _____

**4.** (blue)  sus ojos _____

**5.** (yellow)  el lápiz _____

**6.** (brown)  las blusas _____

**7.** (orange)  la flor _____

**8.** (green)    las frutas _____

**9.** (gray)    los abrigos _____

**10.** (rose)    las camisas _____


# 11 Reading Comprehension [10 points]

Read the following passage and then circle the statement that best answers the question:

Son las cinco de la tarde. Alfredo entra en la tienda. En la calle hace mucho frío. Es el veinte y cuatro de diciembre, el día antes de la Navidad. Necesita comprar un regalo para su mamá. Alfredo dice al hombre que trabaja en la tienda: «Quiero comprar un regalo bonito para mi madre.» «Muy bien», contesta el hombre. «¿Te gusta este sombrero?» «Sí, ¿cuánto cuesta?» «Veinte dólares.» «Es mucho», dice Alfredo. «¿Cuánto dinero tiene?» pregunta el hombre. «Tengo exactamente diez dólares.» «Pues, este suéter cuesta nueve dólares, cincuenta centavos.» «¡Perfecto!» dice Alfredo. «Me gusta mucho. Ahora tengo un regalo bueno para mi mamá.»

1. ¿Qué hora es cuando Alfredo entra en la tienda?
   a. Es la una.  b. Son las diez.  c. Es de noche.  d. Son las cinco.
2. ¿Qué tiempo hace?
   a. Hace buen tiempo.  b. Hace mucho calor.  c. Hace frío.
   d. Hace fresco.
3. Qué quiere comprar Alfredo?
   a. Muchas cosas.  b. Una cosa.  c. Una comida.  d. Un sombrero.
4. ¿Por qué no compra el sombrero?
   a. No tiene el dinero.  b. Quiere una cosa bonita.  c. No le gusta.
   d. No quiere comprar un regalo.
5. ¿Cuánto cuesta el suéter?
   a. Más de diez dólares.  b. Exactamente diez dólares.  c. Menos de diez dólares.  d. Un dólar.

# 12 Slot Completion [5 points]

Read the following passage and then underline the answer that best completes the statement:

Es mediodía. Juan tiene __(1)__. Quiere comer alguna cosa. Va a __(2)__ para hacerse un sandwich. A Juan le gustan la carne y __(3)__. Como postre, come __(4)__. Cuando tiene sed, bebe __(5)__. Es un buen muchacho independiente.

1. (a) frío
   (b) hambre
   (c) miedo
   (d) sueño
2. (a) la cocina
   (b) la sala
   (c) el cuarto de baño
   (d) la casa
3. (a) el dinero
   (b) el helado
   (c) las papas
   (d) el queso
4. (a) sopa
   (b) agua
   (c) pescado
   (d) frutas
5. (a) legumbres
   (b) sol
   (c) jugo
   (d) salchichas

# Vocabulario español-inglés

## A

**a** to, at; **a las dos** at two o'clock
**abierto** open
**abogado** *m.*, **abogada** *f.* lawyer
**abrigo** *m.* coat
**abril** April
**abrir** to open
**abuela** *f.* grandmother
**abuelo** *m.* grandfather; **los abuelos** grandparents
**aceptar** to accept
**actividad** *f.* activity, exercise
**actor** *m.* actor
**actriz** *f.* actress
**adiós** good-bye
**¿adónde?** (to) where?; **¿adónde vas?** where are you going?
**adorar** to adore
**aeropuerto** *m.* airport
**agosto** August
**agua: el agua** *f.* water
**ahora** now
**alegre** happy
**alemán** (*f.* **alemana**) German
**alguna cosa** something
**almacén** *m.* (*pl.* **almacenes**) store
**alumno** *m.*, **alumna** *f.* pupil, student
**allí** there

**amar** to love
**amarillo** yellow
**ambulancia** *f.* ambulance
**americano** (*f.* **americana**) American
**amigo** *m.*, **amiga** *f.* friend
**amor** *m.* love
**anaranjado** orange *(color)*
**animal** *m.* animal; **animal doméstico** pet
**año** *m.*, year; **tener . . . años** to be . . . years old; **¿cuántos años tiene Ud.? ¿cuántos años tienes?** how old are you?
**apartamento** *m.* apartment
**aprender** to learn
**aquí** here
**árbol** *m.* tree
**arreglar** to repair
**arroz** *m.* rice; **arroz con pollo** chicken with rice
**así** so, in this way, thus; **así-así** so-so
**atención** *f.* attention
**ausente** absent
**auto** *m.* car
**autobús** *m.* bus
**automóvil** *m.* automobile
**avenida** *f.* avenue
**avión** *m.* airplane
**¡Ay!** Oh! *(expression of distress)*
**ayudar** to help
**azul** blue

## B

**bailar** to dance
**banana** *f.* banana
**banco** *m.* bank; bench
**bandera** *f.* flag
**barbero** *m.* barber, hairdresser
**beber** to drink
**bicicleta** *f.* bicycle
**bien** well
**biología** *f.* biology
**billete** *m.* ticket
**bistec** *m.* steak
**bizcocho** *m.* biscuit, cake
**blanco** white
**blusa** *f.* blouse
**boca** *f.* mouth
**bolso** *m.* purse, bag
**bonito** pretty
**bota** *f.* boot
**brazo** *m.* arm
**bueno** good; all right, O.K. **¡Qué bueno!** How nice!
**buscar** to look for

## C

**caballo** *m.* horse
**cabeza** *f.* head
**caer(se)** to fall (down)
**café** *m.* coffee; coffee house
**calcetín** *m.* sock
**cálculo** *m.* calculation; **hacer cálculos** to calculate; to do math

**401**

**calendario** *m.* calendar
**caliente** warm, hot
**calor** *m.* heat; **hacer calor** to be warm/hot *(weather)*; **tener calor** to be (= feel) warm/hot
**calle** *f.* street
**cama** *f.* bed
**camarero** *m.* waiter
**camello** *m.* camel
**camisa** *f.* shirt
**campamento** *m.* camp
**campista** *m.&f.* camper
**cansado** tired
**cantar** to sing
**capaz** capable
**cara** *f.* face
**¡Caramba!** Well! Goodness gracious! Gosh!
**carne** *m.* meat; **carne de vaca** beef
**carpintero** *m.* carpenter
**cartero** *m.* mailman, letter carrier
**casa** *f.* house, home; **en casa** at home
**castaño** brown
**catorce** fourteen
**celebrar** to celebrate
**cena** *f.* supper
**centavo** *m.* cent, penny
**cereal** *m.* cereal
**cien, ciento** one hundred
**ciencia** *f.* science; **ciencia ficción** science fiction
**cierto** true; **¿no es cierto?** isn't it?
**cinco** five
**cincuenta** fifty
**cine** *m.* movie theater; **ir al cine** to go to the movies
**ciudad** *f.* city
**claro** of course; **claro que no** of course not, no way

**clase** *f.* class; classroom; kind, type; **la clase de español** Spanish class; **no hay clases hoy** there's no school today; **muchas clases de** many kinds of; **¿qué clase de?** what kind of?
**cocina** *f.* kitchen
**cochino** *m.* pig
**colombiano** (*f.* **colombiana**) Columbian
**color** *m.* color
**combatir** to combat, to fight
**comedor** *m.* dining room
**comer** to eat
**cómico** funny
**comida** *f.* meal; food
**como** as, like, **¿cómo?** how?; **¿Cómo estás? ¿Cómo está Ud.?** How are you?
**comprar** to buy
**comprender** to understand
**computador** *m.* computer
**con** with
**concurso** *m.* contest
**confortable** comfortable
**consejero** *m.* counselor
**conmigo** with me; **contigo** with you
**contar** to count; **yo cuento** I count
**contento** glad, happy
**contestar** to answer
**conversación** *f.* conversation
**corbata** *f.* necktie
**correo** *m.* post office
**correr** to run
**cosa** *f.* thing
**costar** to cost; **cuesta** it costs

**creer** to believe; **creo que no** I don't think so
**crucigrama** *f.* crossword puzzle
**cuaderno** *m.* notebook
**¿cuál ¿cuáles?** which? what?
**cuando** when; **¿cuándo?** when?
**¿cuánto?** how much? **¿cuántos?** how many
**cuarenta** forty
**cuarto** *m.* room; **cuarto de baño** bathroom
**cuarto** fourth; quarter
**cuatro** four
**cubano** *m.*, **cubana** *f.* Cuban
**cubrir** to cover
**cuerpo** *m.* body
**cuidar** to look after
**cultura** *f.* culture
**cumpleaños** *m.* birthday

**CH**

**chaqueta** *f.* jacket
**chocolate** *m.* chocolate

**D**

**dar** to give; **yo doy** I give
**de** of, from; **la hermana de María** Maria's sister
**deber** must
**decidir** to decide
**decir** to say, to tell
**dedo** *m.* finger
**delicioso** delicious
**dentista** *m.&f.* dentist
**deporte** *m.* sport
**derecho** right
**descripción** *f.* description
**desear** to wish, to want
**después de** after

**destruir** to destroy

**día** *m.* day; **buenos días** good morning; **día de fiesta** holiday; **todo el día** all day; **todos los días** every day

**diálogo** *m.* dialog

**diccionario** *m.* dictionary

**diciembre** December

**dictador** *m.* dictator

**diez** ten; **diez y nueve** nineteen; **diez y ocho** eighteen; **diez y seis** sixteen; **diez y siete** seventeen

**diferente** different

**difícil** difficult, hard

**dinero** *m.* money

**Dios** God

**director** *m.*, **directora** *f.* director; (school) principal

**disco** *m.* phonograph record

**discoteca** *f.* discotheque, disco

**disfraz** *m.* costume; **la fiesta de disfraces** costume party

**divertido** amusing

**dividido por** divided by

**dividir** to divide

**doce** twelve

**docena** *f.* dozen

**doctor** *m.*, **doctora** *f.* doctor

**dólar** *m.* dollar

**dolor** *m.* pain, ache; **tener dolor de oído** to have an earache

**domingo** *m.* Sunday

**¿dónde?** where?

**dormir** to sleep

**dormitorio** *m.* bedroom

**dos** two

**dragón** *m.* dragon

**durante** during

### E

**edad** *f.* age

**ejercicio** *m.* exercise

**el** the

**él** he

**elefante** *m.* elephant

**elegante** elegant, stylish

**ella** she

**ellos** *m.*, **ellas** *f.* they

**enero** January

**enfermedad** *f.* illness, sickness

**enfermero** *m.*, **enfermera** *f.* nurse

**enfermo** sick, ill

**ensalada** *f.* salad

**entonces** then; in that case

**entrar (en)** to enter; **entrar en la clase** to enter (come into) the class

**entre** among, between

**entrevista** *f.* interview

**escribir** to write

**escuchar** to listen (to)

**escolar: año escolar** school year

**escuela** *f.* school

**esa, ese, eso** that; **por eso** for that reason

**español** Spanish; **español** *m.* Spanish (language); **español** *m.*, **española** *f.* Spaniard

**especial** special

**especialidad** *f.* specialty

**esquiar** to ski

**estación** *f.* season; station

**estar** to be; **está bien** O.K., all right

**este, esta** this; **esta noche** tonight

**estricto** strict

**estudiante** *m. & f.* student

**estudiar** to study

**estupendo** marvelous, terrific

**estúpido** stupid

**exactamente, ¡exacto!** exactly

**examen** *m.* (*pl.* **exámenes**) examination, test

**examinar** to examine

**excelente** excellent

**extraordinario** extraordinary

### F

**fabuloso** fabulous

**fácil** easy

**falda** *f.* skirt

**falso** false

**familia** *f.* family

**famoso** famous

**fantástico** fantastic

**farmacia** *f.* pharmacy, drugstore

**favor** *m.* favor; **por favor** please

**favorito** favorite

**febrero** February

**fecha** *f.* date

**feo** ugly

**feroz** ferocious, fierce

**fiesta** *f.* party

**fin** *m.* end

**finalmente** finally

**flaco** thin, skinny

**flor** *f.* flower

**fotografía** *f.* photograph

**francés** (*f.* **francesa**) French; **francés** *m.* Frenchman, **francesa** *f.* Frenchwoman

**fresco** fresh; **hace fresco** it's cool/chilly *(weather)*

**frío** cold; **hacer frío** to be cold *(weather);* **tener frío** to be (= feel) cold; **estar frío** to be cold *(liquids or objects)*

**fruta** *f.* fruit

**fuerte** strong

**fútbol** *m.* football

### G

**galopar** to gallop

**gallina** *f.* hen

**ganar** to win; to earn

**garaje** *m.* garage

**garganta** *f.* throat

**gasolina** *f.* gasoline, gas

**gatito** *m.* kitten

**gato** *m.* cat

**general** *m.* general

**generalmente** in general

**gigante** *m.* giant

**gordo** fat

**gracias** thanks, thank you; **muchas gracias** thanks very much

**grabadora** *f.* cassette player

**grande** big, large, great

**gripe** *f.* flu

**gris** grey

**gritar** to cry out

**guante** *m.* glove

**guapo** handsome

**gustar** to please (someone): **me gusta(n)** I like

### H

**habitante** *m.* inhabitant

**hablar** to speak, to talk

**hacer** to do, to make; **hace buen tiempo** the weather is nice; **hace calor** it's warm/hot; **hace fresco** it's cool/chilly; **hace frío** it's cold; **hace mal tiempo** the weather is bad; **hace sol** it's sunny; **hace viento** it's windy; **¿Qué tiempo hace?** How's the weather?

**hambre: el hambre** *f.* hunger; **tener hambre** to be hungry

**hamburguesa** *f.* hamburger

**hasta** until; **hasta la vista** I'll be seeing you, see you later; **hasta mañana** see you tomorrow; **hasta luego** so long

**hay** there is, there are; **no hay** there isn't, there aren't

**helado** *m.* ice cream; **helado de vainilla** vanilla ice cream

**hermana** *f.* sister

**hermano** *m.* brother

**hija** *f.* daughter

**hijo** *m.* son; **los hijos** sons, son(s) and daughter(s)

**historia** *f.* history

**hola** hello, hi

**hombre** *m.* man

**hora** *f.* hour; **¿Qué hora es?** What time is it?

**hospital** *m.* hospital

**hotel** *m.* hotel

**hoy** today

**huevo** *m.* egg; **huevos duros** hard-boiled eggs

### I

**idea** *f.* idea

**iglesia** *f.* church

**imaginación** *f.* imagination

**importa: no importa** it doesn't matter, never mind

**importante** important

**imposible** impossible

**independiente** independent

**información** *f.* information

**inglés** *m.* English

**inmediatamente** immediately

**insecto** *m.* insect

**inteligente** intelligent

**interesante** interesting

**invierno** *m.* winter

**invitado** invited

**invitar** to invite

**ir** to go

**italiano** Italian

### J

**jardín** *f.* garden

**joven** *(pl.* **jóvenes)** young

**jueves** *m.* Thursday

**jugar** to play *(games)*

**jugo** *m.* juice; **jugo de naranja** orange juice

**julio** July

**jungla** *f.* jungle

**junio** June

### L

**la** *(pl.* **las)** the

**laboratorio** *m.* laboratory

**lámpara** *f.* lamp

**lanzar** to throw

**lápiz** *m. (pl.* **lápices)** pencil

**largo** long

**lección** *f.* lesson

**leche** *f.* milk
**lechuga** *f.* lettuce
**leer** to read
**legumbre** *f.* vegetable
**lengua** *f.* tongue, language
**león** *m.* lion
**libro** *m.* book
**loco (por)** crazy (about)
**lodo** *m.* mud
**lotería** *f.* lottery
**los** the
**lugar** *m.* place
**lunes** *m.* Monday

## LL

**llamar** to call; **¿Cómo te llamas?, ¿Cómo se llama Ud.?** What is your name?; **yo me llamo Susana** my name is Susan; **él se llama Pablo** his name is Paul
**llegar** to arrive
**llevar** to wear
**llover** to rain; **va a llover** it's going to rain; **llueve** it's raining, it rains

## M

**madre** *f.* mother; **¡Madre mía!** My goodness!
**magnífico** splendid, wonderful
**mal, malo** bad
**mamá** *f.* mother, mom
**mano** *f.* hand
**mañana** tomorrow; **de la mañana** A.M., in the morning
**martes** *m.* Tuesday
**marzo** March
**más** more; **más de, más que** more than; **no**

**puede . . . más** he can . . . no longer
**matemáticas** *f. pl.* mathematics
**mayo** May
**mecánico** *m.* mechanic
**medalla** *f.* medal
**media** *f.* stocking; sock
**medianoche** *f.* midnight
**medicina** *f.* medicine
**médico** *m.,* **médica** *f.* physician, doctor
**medio** half; **es la una y media** it is half past one (o'clock)
**mediodía** *m.* noon
**menos** minus
**menú** *m.* menu
**mercado** *m.* market
**mes** *m.* month
**mesa** *f.* table; desk
**método** *m.* method
**mexicano** *m.,* **mexicana** *f.* Mexican
**mi, mis** my
**miedo** *m.* fear; **tener miedo** to be afraid
**miembro** *m.* member
**miércoles** *m.* Wednesday
**mirar** to look (at); **mirar la televisión** to watch television
**mixto** mixed
**moderno** modern
**mono** *m.* monkey, ape
**moreno** dark
**mosquito** *m.* mosquito
**muchacha** *f.* girl
**muchacho** *m.* boy
**mucho** much, a great deal (of), a lot (of); **muchos** many; **tengo mucho calor** I'm very warm
**mueca** *f.* grimace; **hacer muecas** to make faces

**mujer** *f.* woman
**mundo** *m.* world; **todo el mundo** everybody
**música** *f.* music
**muy** very

## N

**nacionalidad** *f.* nationality
**nada** nothing; **de nada** you're welcome
**naranja** *f.* orange
**nariz** *f.* nose
**naturalmente** naturally
**Navidad** *f.* Christmas
**necesario** necessary
**necesitar** to need
**negro** black
**nena** *f.* baby girl
**nieva** it is snowing, it snows
**nieve** *f.* snow; **la bola de nieve** snowball; **la figura de nieve** snowman
**niño** *m.,* **niña** *f.* child
**no** no, not
**noche** *f.* night; **buenas noches** good evening; good night; **todas las noches** every night; **de la noche** P.M., in the evening, at night
**nosotros** *m.,* **nosotras** *f.* we
**noventa** ninety
**noviembre** November
**nuestro, nuestra** our
**nueve** nine
**nuevo** new
**número** *m.* number; **número de teléfono** telephone number
**nunca** never

## O

**o** or
**octubre** October
**ochenta** eighty
**ocho** eight
**odiar** to hate
**oficina** *f.* office
**ojo** *m.* eye; **ojos pardos** brown eyes
**once** eleven
**orden** *m.* order
**ordinario** ordinary
**oreja** *f.* ear
**otoño** *m.* autumn, fall
**otro, otra, otros, otras** other, another

## P

**paciente** *m.&f.* patient
**padre** *m.* father; **los padres** parents
**pan** *m.* bread
**pantalones** *m. pl.* pants, trousers
**papa** *f.* potato; **papas fritas** french fried potatoes; **el puré de papas** mashed potatoes
**papel** *m.* paper
**par** *m.* pair
**para** for; to, in order to
**pardo** brown
**parecerse** to resemble; **se parece a** it resembles
**parque** *m.* park; **parque zoológico** zoo
**parte** *f.* part, section
**partido** *m.* match
**pasar** to pass; to happen; **¿qué te pasa?** what's the matter with you?
**pasear** to take for a walk
**pastel** *m.* cake
**pata** *f.* paw

**pato** *m.* duck
**película** *f.* film, movie
**pelo** *m.* hair
**pensar (en)** to think (of); **yo pienso** I think
**pequeño** small
**perfecto** perfect
**periódico** *m.* newspaper
**pero** but
**perro** *m.*, **perra** *f.* dog
**persona** *f.* person
**personal** personal
**personaje** *m.* character (*in a play*)
**pescado** *m.* fish (*after it's been caught*)
**pez** *m.* fish (*alive and swimming*)
**piano** *m.* piano
**pie** *m.* foot
**pierna** *f.* leg
**pizarra** *f.* blackboard, chalkboard
**plástico** plastic
**plato** *m.* plate, dish
**playa** *f.* beach
**pluma** *f.* pen
**pobre** poor
**poco** little (in quantity); **un poco de agua** a little water; **pocos** few
**poema** *m.* poem
**policía** *m.* policeman
**pollo** *m.* chicken
**por** by, through (in exchange) for; "times" (x); **dividido por** divided by; **por eso** for that reason; **¿por qué?** why?
**porque** because
**postre** *m.* dessert
**portátil** portable
**practicar** to practice
**precio** *m.* price; **a precios bajos** at low prices

**preferir** to prefer; **yo prefiero** I prefer
**pregunta** *f.* question
**preguntar** to ask
**premio** *m.* prize
**preocuparse** to worry; **no te preocupes** don't worry
**preparado** prepared
**preparar** to prepare
**presidente** *m.*, **presidenta** *f.* president
**primavera** *f.* spring(time)
**primer, primero** first
**princesa** *f.* princess
**principal** principal, main
**probablemente** probably
**problema** *m.* problem
**profesor** *m.*, **profesora** *f.* teacher
**programa** *m.* program
**proponer** to propose
**pueblo** *m.* town
**puerta** *f.* door
**pues** well, then
**puré** *m.* **de papas** mashed potatoes

## Q

**que** that, than; **más que** more than; **¿qué?** what? which?; **¡Qué trabajo!** What a job!
**querer** to want
**querido** dear
**queso** *m.* cheese
**¿quién? ¿quiénes?** who?
**quince** fifteen
**quinto** fifth

## R

**radio** *m.&f.* radio
**rápido** fast, rapid; **rápidamente** fast, rapidly

**razón** *f.* reason, right; **tener razón** to be right; **no tener razón** to be wrong

**recibir** to receive

**regalo** *m.* gift, present

**regla** *f.* ruler; rule

**regular** regular; so-so

**reloj** *m.* clock, watch

**repórter** *m.* reporter

**resfriado** *m.* cold; **tener un resfriado** to have a cold

**responder** to respond, to answer, to reply

**responsabilidad** *f.* responsibility

**respuesta** *f.* answer

**restaurante** *m.* restaurant

**rico** rich

**rojo** red

**romántico** romantic

**ropa** *f.* clothes, clothing

**rosa** *f.* rose

**rosado** rose (*color*)

**rubio** blond

**ruidoso** noisy

### S

**sábado** *m.* Saturday

**saber** to know; to know how; **yo sé** I know

**sala** *f.* living room

**salchicha** *f.* sausage, frankfurter

**salir** to leave, to go out; **yo salgo** I leave; **salir de la casa** to leave the house

**sandwich** *m.* sandwich

**sección** *f.* section

**secretario** *m.*, **secretaria** *f.* secretary

**sed** *f.* thirst; **tener sed** to be thirsty

**segundo** second

**seis** six

**semana** *f.* week

**sentado** seated

**sentir** to feel; **lo siento** I'm sorry

**señor** *m.* Mr.; **señores** *m. pl.* Mr. and Mrs.; sir, madam

**señora** *f.* lady; Mrs.

**señorita** *f.* young lady; Miss

**septiembre** September

**ser** to be

**serio** serious

**sesenta** sixty

**setenta** seventy

**si** if

**sí** yes

**siempre** always

**siete** seven

**silla** *f.* chair

**simpático** nice

**sin** without

**sobre** on, on top of; about, regarding

**soda** *f.* soda

**sofá** *m.* sofa

**socio** *m.*, **socia** *f.* associate

**sol** *m.* sun; **hace sol** (*or* **hay sol**) it's sunny

**sólo, solamente** only

**sombrero** *m.* hat

**sopa** *f.* soup

**sorpresa** *f.* surprise; **la fiesta de sorpresa** surprise party

**su, sus** your, his, her, their

**sueño** *m.* sleep; **tener sueño** to be sleepy

**suerte** *f.* luck; **¡Buena suerte!** Good luck!

**suéter** *m.* sweater

**sufrir** to suffer

**sumar** to add (up)

**supermercado** *m.* supermarket

**supuesto: por supuesto** of course

### T

**también** also, too

**tan** so

**tarde** late; **más tarde** later; **se hace tarde** it's getting late

**tarde** *f.* afternoon; **buenas tardes** good afternoon; **de la tarde** P.M., in the afternoon

**tarea** *f.* task, homework, assignment; (*pl.*) homework (*all homework assignments for a given day*)

**taxi** *m.* taxi, cab

**teatro** *m.* theater

**telefonista** *m. & f.* telephone operator

**teléfono** *m.* telephone

**televisión** *f.* television; **mirar la televisión** to watch television

**tener** to have; **tener . . . años** to be . . . years old; **tener calor** to be (= feel) warm/hot; **tener frío** to be (= feel) cold; **tener hambre** to be hungry; **tener razón** to be right; **no tener razón** to be wrong; **tener sed** to be thirsty; **tener sueño** to be sleepy

**terminar** to end, to finish

**tenis** *m.* tennis

**tercero** third

**tía** *f.* aunt
**tiempo** *m.* time; weather;
  **¿qué tiempo hace?**
  how's the weather?
**tienda** *f.* store
**tigre** *m.* tiger
**tímido** shy, timid
**todavía** still
**todo** everything; **todos,**
  **todas** all (of them);
  **todo el día** all day; **todo**
  **el mundo** everybody;
  **todos los días** every day
**tomar** to take
**tomate** *m.* tomato
**trabajar** to work; **trabajar**
  **mucho** to work hard
**trabajo** *m.* work
**traje** *m.* suit; dress
**transformar** to transform
**transporte** *m.* transportation
**trece** thirteen
**treinta** thirty
**tren** *m.* train
**tres** three
**triste** sad
**tropical** tropical
**tú** you (*familiar*)
**tu, tus** your (*familiar*)

## U

**último** last
**un, una** a, one; **uno** (number) one; **unos, unas**
  some, a few
**usado** used
**usar** to use
**usted (Ud.)** you (*formal*
  *singular*); **ustedes (Uds.)**
  you (*plural*)

## V

**vaca** *f.* cow
**vacaciones** *f. (pl.)* vacation
**vainilla** *f.* vanilla
**¡vamos! (!vámonos!)** let's
  go!
**varios** several
**vaso** *m.* (drinking) glass
**vegetariano** vegetarian
**veinte** twenty
**vendaje** *m.* bandage
**vendedor** *m.* salesman,
  seller
**vender** to sell
**ventana** *f.* window
**ver** to see; **yo veo** I see

**verano** *m.* summer(time)
**verdad** *f.* truth; **es verdad**
  it's true; **¿verdad?** isn't
  it so?
**verde** green
**vestido** *m.* dress
**vez** *f.* (*pl.* **veces**) time;
  **otra vez** again; **la**
  **segunda vez** the second
  time
**viejo** old
**viento** *m.* wind; **hace**
  **viento** it's windy
**viernes** *m.* Friday
**visitar** to visit
**vivir** to live
**vocabulario** *m.* vocabulary

## Y

**y** and; plus
**yo** I

## Z

**zapatería** *f.* shoe store;
  shoemaker's shop
**zapato** *m.* shoe
**zoológico** *m.* zoo

# Vocabulario inglés-español

## A

**a, an** un, una
**about** sobre, de
**absent** ausente
**accept** aceptar
**activity** actividad *f.*
**actor** actor *m.*
**actress** actriz *f.*
**add (up)** sumar
**adore** adorar
**afraid: to be afraid** tener miedo
**after** después de
**afternoon** tarde *f.*; **good afternoon** buenas tardes
**again** otra vez
**age** edad *f.*
**airplane** avión *m.*
**airport** aeropuerto *m.*
**all (of them)** todos, todas
**also** también
**always** siempre
**ambulance** ambulancia *f.*
**American** americano *m.*, americana *f.*
**among** entre
**amusing** divertido
**and** y
**animal** animal *m.*
**answer** respuesta *f.*; contestar, responder
**apartment** apartamento *m.*
**April** abril

**arm** brazo *m.*
**arrive** llegar
**ask** preguntar
**associate** socio *m.*, socia *f.*
**at** a; **at home** en casa; **at one o'clock** a la una; **at two o'clock** a las dos; **at what time?** ¿a qué hora?
**attention** atención *f.*
**August** agosto
**aunt** tía *f.*
**automobile** automóvil *m.*
**autumn** otoño *m.*
**avenue** avenida *f.*

## B

**baby** nene *m.*, nena *f.*, bebé *m.*
**bad** mal, malo
**bag** bolso *m.*
**banana** banana *f.*
**bandage** vendaje *m.*
**bank** banco *m.*
**barber** barbero *m.*
**bathroom** cuarto de baño *m.*
**be** ser, estar; **to be cold** estar frío; *(= to feel cold)* tener frío; *(weather)* hacer frío; **to be warm** estar caliente; *(= to feel warm)* tener calor; *(weather)* hacer calor; **to be hungry** tener hambre;

**to be thirsty** tener sed;
**to be . . . years old** tener . . . años; **I am ten years old** tengo diez años
**beach** playa *f.*
**because** porque
**bed** cama *f.*
**bedroom** dormitorio *m.*
**bench** banco *m.*
**between** entre
**bicycle** bicicleta *f.*
**big** grande
**biology** biología *f.*
**birthday** cumpleaños *m.*
**biscuit** bizcocho *m.*
**black** negro
**blackboard** pizarra *f.*
**blond** rubio
**blouse** blusa *f.*
**blue** azul
**body** cuerpo *m.*
**book** libro *m.*
**boot** bota *f.*
**boy** muchacho *m.*
**bread** pan *m.*
**brother** hermano *m.*; **brother(s) and sister(s)** los hermanos
**brown** pardo, castaño, café; **brown eyes** los ojos pardos
**bus** autobús *m.*
**but** pero
**buy** comprar

## C

**cab** taxi *m.*
**cake** pastel *m.*
**calculate** hacer cálculos, calcular
**calculation** cálculo *m.*
**calendar** calendario *m.*
**call** llamar
**camel** camello *m.*
**camp** campamento *m.*
**camper** campista *m.&f.*
**capable** capaz
**car** auto *m.*, coche *m.*
**carpenter** carpintero *m.*
**cassette player** grabadora *f.*
**cat** gato *m.*
**celebrate** celebrar
**cereal** cereal *m.*
**cent** centavo *m.*
**chair** silla *f.*
**character** *(in play)* personaje *m.*
**cheese** queso *m.*
**chicken** pollo *m.*
**child** niño *m.* niña *f.*, **children** los niños
**chilly: it is chilly** hace fresco
**chocolate** chocolate *m.;* **chocolate ice cream** el helado de chocolate
**Christmas** Navidad *f.*
**church** iglesia *f.*
**city** ciudad *f.*
**class** clase *f.;* **in class** en la clase
**clock** reloj *m.*
**clothes, clothing** ropa *f.*
**coat** abrigo *m.*
**coffee** café *m.*
**cold** frío; **to be cold** estar frío; *(= to feel cold)* tener frío; *(weather)* hacer frío; **to have a cold** tener un resfriado

**Columbian** colombiano, *m.* colombiana *f.*
**color** color *m.*
**comfortable** confortable
**computer** computador *m.*
**contest** concurso *m.*
**conversation** conversación *f.*
**cool** fresco; **it's cool** *(weather)* hace fresco
**cost** precio *m.;* costar; **it costs** cuesta
**costume** disfraz *m.;* **costume party** la fiesta de disfraces
**counselor** consejero *m.*
**count** contar; **I count** yo cuento
**course: of course** por supuesto
**cover** cubrir
**cow** vaca *f.*
**crazy** loco
**crossword puzzle** crucigrama *m.*
**cry out** gritar
**Cuban** cubano *m.*, cubana *f.*
**culture** cultura *f.*

## D

**dance** bailar
**dark** *(person)* moreno
**date** fecha *f.*
**daughter** hija *f.*
**day** día *m.*
**dear** querido
**December** diciembre
**decide** decidir
**delicious** delicioso
**dentist** dentista *m.&f.*
**description** descripción *f.*
**desk** mesa *f.*
**dessert** postre *m.*
**destroy** destruir
**dialog** diálogo *m.*

**dictator** dictador *m.*
**dictionary** diccionario *m.*
**different** diferente
**difficult** difícil
**dining room** comedor *m.*
**disco** discoteca *f.*
**dish** plato *m.*
**divide** dividir; **divided by** dividido por
**do** hacer; **to do the homework** hacer la(s) tarea(s)
**doctor** doctor *m.*, doctora *f.;* médico *m.*, médica *f.*
**dog** perro *m.*, perra *f.*
**dollar** dólar *m.*
**door** puerta *f.*
**dozen** docena *f.*
**dragon** dragón *m.*
**dress** vestido *m.;* traje *m.*
**drink** bebida *f.;* beber
**drugstore** farmacia *f.*
**duck** pato *m.*
**during** durante

## E

**ear** oreja *f.* , oído *m.*
**earache** dolor *(m.)* de oído
**earn** ganar
**easy** fácil
**eat** comer
**egg** huevo *m.;* **hard-boiled eggs** huevos duros
**eight** ocho
**eighteen** diez y ocho
**eighty** ochenta
**elegant** elegante
**elephant** elefante *m.*
**eleven** once
**end** fin *m.;* terminar
**English** inglés *m.*
**enter** entrar
**everybody** todo el mundo
**everything** todo
**exactly** exactamente, ¡exacto!

**examination** examen *m.*
**examine** examinar
**excellent** excelente
**exercise** ejercicio *m.*
**extraordinary** extraordinario
**eye** ojo *m.*

**F**

**fabulous** fabuloso
**face** cara *f.*; **to make faces** hacer muecas
**fall** otoño *m.*, **to fall (down)** caer(se)
**false** falso
**family** familia *f.*
**famous** famoso
**fantastic** fantástico
**fast** rápido, rápidamente
**fat** gordo
**father** padre *m.*
**favorite** favorito
**February** febrero
**ferocious** feroz
**fifteen** quince
**fifth** quinto
**fifty** cincuenta
**fight** combatir
**finally** finalmente
**finger** dedo *m.*
**first** primer, primero
**fish** pescado *m.*; pez *m.* *(when it's alive)*
**five** cinco
**fifteen** quince
**fifth** quinto
**fifty** cincuenta
**flag** bandera *f.*
**flower** flor *f.*
**food** comida *f.*
**foot** pie *m.*
**football** fútbol *m.*
**forty** cuarenta
**four** cuatro
**fourteen** catorce
**fourth** cuarto

**French** francés *m.;*
**Frenchman** francés *m.;*
**Frenchwoman** francesa *f.*
**french fries** las papas fritas
**Friday** viernes *m.*
**friend** amigo *m.*, amiga *f.*
**from** de
**fruit** fruta *f.*
**funny** cómico

**G**

**gallop** galopar
**garage** garaje *m.*
**garden** jardín *m.*
**gasoline** gasolina *f.*
**general** general *m.;* **in general** generalmente
**German** alemán *m.;* alemán *m.*, alemana *f.*
**giant** gigante *m.*
**gift** regalo *m.*
**girl** muchacha *f.*
**give** dar; **I give** yo doy
**glass** vaso *m.,;* **glass of milk** vaso de leche
**go** ir; **to go in(to)** entrar en; **to be going to (do something)** ir a + *inf.:* **I'm going to read** voy a
**good** bueno; **good morning** buenos días; **good afternoon** buenas tardes; **good evening, good night** buenas noches
**good-bye** adiós
**grandfather** abuelo *m.*
**grandmother** abuela *f.*
**grandparents** los abuelos
**green** verde
**grey** gris

**H**

**hair** pelo *m.*
**half** medio; **half past one**

la una y media
**hamburger** hamburguesa *f.*
**hand** mano *f.*
**handsome** guapo
**happy** contento, alegre; **to be happy** estar contento, estar alegre
**hard** difícil; **to work hard** trabajar mucho
**hat** sombrero *m.*
**hate** odiar
**have** tener
**he** él
**head** cabeza *f.*
**hello** hola
**help** ayudar
**hen** gallina *f.*
**her** su, sus
**here** aquí
**his** su, sus
**history** historia *f.*
**holiday** día de fiesta *m.* *(pl.* los días de fiesta)
**home: to be (at) home** estar en casa; **to go home** ir a casa
**homework assignment** tarea *f.*
**horrible** horrible
**horse** caballo *m.*
**hospital** hospital *m.*
**hot** (muy) caliente; **to be hot** estar muy caliente; *(= to feel hot)* tener mucho calor; *(weather)* hacer mucho calor
**hotel** hotel *m.*
**house** casa *f.*
**how?** ¿cómo?; **how are you?** ¿cómo está Ud.? ¿cómo estás?; **how much?** ¿cuánto?; **how many?** ¿cuántos?
**hundred** cien, ciento; **a hundred dollars** cien dólares; **one hundred**

**fifty dollars** ciento cincuenta dólares
**hungry: to be hungry** tener hambre

**I**

**I** yo
**idea** idea *f.*
**ice cream** helado *m.*
**if** si
**illness** enfermedad *f.*
**important** importante
**impossible** imposible
**in** en
**independent** independiente
**information** información *f.*
**inhabitant** habitante *m.*
**insect** insecto *m.*
**intelligent** inteligente
**interesting** interesante
**invite** invitar; **invited** invitado
**it** *(subject)* él, ella
**Italian** italiano

**J**

**jacket** chaqueta *f.*
**January** enero
**juice** jugo *m.;* **orange juice** jugo de naranja
**July** julio
**jungle** jungla *f.*
**June** junio

**K**

**kitchen** cocina *f.*
**kitten** gatito *m.*
**know** saber; **I know** yo sé; **to know how to** *(do something)* saber + *inf.;* **she knows how to sing** ella sabe cantar

**L**

**laboratory** laboratorio *m.*
**lady** señora *f.*
**lamp** lámpara *f.*
**language** lengua *f.*
**large** grande
**last** último
**late** tarde; **it's getting late** se hace tarde
**lawyer** abogado *m.,* abogada *f.*
**learn** aprender
**leave** salir; **I leave** yo salgo; **to leave school** salir de la escuela
**leg** pierna *f.*
**lesson** lección *f.*
**letter** carta *f.;* **letter carrier** cartero *m.*
**lettuce** lechuga *f.*
**like: I like the book** me gusta el libro; **do you like the photos?** ¿te gustan las fotos?
**lion** león *m.*
**listen (to)** escuchar
**little** *(in size)* pequeño; *(in quantity)* poco
**live** vivir
**living room** sala *f.*
**long** largo; **he can . . . no longer** no puede . . . más
**look (at)** mirar
**look after** cuidar
**look for** buscar
**lot: a lot (of)** mucho; **lots of** muchos
**lottery** lotería *f.*
**love** amar; amor *m.*

**M**

**mailman** cartero *m.*
**main** principal
**man** hombre *m.*

**many** muchos, muchas
**March** marzo
**market** mercado *m.*
**marvelous** estupendo, maravilloso
**mashed potatoes** el puré de papas
**match** partido *m.*
**mathematics** matemáticas *f. pl.;* **to do math** calcular
**matter: it doesn't matter** no importa
**May** mayo
**meal** comida *f.*
**meat** carne *f.*
**mechanic** mecánico *m.*
**medal** medalla *f.*
**medicine** medicina *f.*
**member** miembro *m.*
**menu** menú *m.*
**method** método *m.*
**Mexican** mexicano *m.,* mexicana *f.*
**midnight** medianoche *f.*
**milk** leche *f.*
**minus** menos
**Miss** señorita *f.*
**mixed** mixto
**modern** moderno
**mom** mamá *f.*
**Monday** lunes *m.*
**money** dinero *m.*
**monkey** mono *m.*
**month** mes *m.*
**more** más
**morning** mañana *f.;* **good morning** buenos días
**mosquito** mosquito *m.*
**mother** madre *f.,* mamá *f.*
**mouth** boca *f.*
**movie** película *f.*
**movies** cine *m.;* **to go to the movies** ir al cine
**Mr.** señor *m.*
**Mrs.** señora *f.*

**music** música *f.*
**must** deber
**my** mi, mis

## N

**name** nombre *m.;* **what's your name?** *(familiar)* ¿cómo te llamas?, *(formal)* ¿cómo se llama Ud.?; **my name is Maria** (yo) me llamo María; **what's his (her) name?** ¿cómo se llama él (ella)?; **his (her) name is** . . . se llama . . . ; **their names are** . . . se llaman . . .
**nationality** nacionalidad *f.*
**natural** natural; **naturally** naturalmente
**necessary** necesario
**necktie** corbata *f.*
**need** necesitar
**never** nunca
**new** nuevo
**newspaper** periódico *m.*
**nice** buen, bueno; *(person)* amable, simpático
**night** noche *f.;* **good night** buenas noches
**nine** nueve
**nineteen** diez y nueve
**ninety** noventa
**no, not** no
**noisy** ruidoso
**noon** mediodía *m.*
**nose** nariz *f.*
**notebook** cuaderno *m.*
**nothing** nada
**November** noviembre
**now** ahora
**number** número *m;* **telephone number** número de teléfono
**nurse** enfermero *m.,* enfermera *f.*

## O

**o'clock: at one o'clock** a la una; **at two o'clock (three o'clock,** *etc.***)** a las dos (las tres, *etc.*)
**October** octubre
**of** de
**of course** claro; **of course not** claro que no
**office** oficina *f.*
**old** viejo; **how old are you?** ¿cuántos años tiene Ud.? ¿cuántos años tienes? **I am fifteen years old** tengo quince años
**on** en, sobre
**one** uno, una
**one hundred** cien, ciento
**only** sólo, solamente
**open** abrir; **the door is open** la puerta está abierta
**or** o
**orange** naranja *f.; (color)* anaranjado; **orange juice** jugo *(m.)* de naranja
**order** orden *m.*
**ordinary** ordinario
**original** original
**other** otro, otra, otros, otras
**our** nuestro, nuestra

## P

**pain** dolor *m.*
**pair** par *m.*
**pants** pantalones *m. pl.*
**paper** papel *m.*
**parents** padres *m. pl.*
**park** parque *m.*
**part** parte *f.*
**party** fiesta *f.*
**pass** pasar

**patient** paciente *m.&f.*
**paw** pata *f.*
**pen** pluma *f.*
**pencil** lápiz *m.* (*pl.* lápices)
**penny** centavo *m.*
**perfect** perfecto
**person** persona *f.*
**personal** personal
**pet** animal doméstico *m.*
**pharmacy** farmacia *f.*
**photograph** fotografía *f.*
**piano** piano *m.*
**pig** cochino *m.*
**place** lugar *m.*
**plastic** plástico
**plate** plato *m.*
**play** jugar
**please** por favor
**plus** y
**poem** poema *m.*
**policeman** policía *m.*
**poor** pobre
**popular** popular
**portable** portátil
**post office** correo *m.*
**potato** papa *f.;* **french fried potatoes** papas fritas; **mashed potatoes** el puré de papas
**practice** practicar
**prefer** preferir; **I prefer** yo prefiero
**prepare** preparar; **prepared** preparado
**present** regalo *m.*
**president** presidente *m.,* presidenta *f.*
**pretty** bonito
**price** precio *m.*
**princess** princesa *f.*
**principal** *(school)* director *m.,* directora *f.*
**prize** premio *m.*
**probably** probablemente
**problem** problema *m.*
**program** programa *m.*

## Q

**quarter: a quarter past one** la una y cuarto
**question** pregunta *f.*; **to ask a question** hacer una pregunta

## R

**radio** radio *m.&f.*
**rain** llover; **it's raining, it rains** llueve
**read** leer
**receive** recibir
**record** disco *m.*
**red** rojo
**repair** arreglar
**reporter** repórter *m.*
**resemble** parecerse; **it resembles** se parece a
**responsibility** reponsabilidad *f.*
**restaurant** restaurante *m.*
**rice** arroz *m.*
**rich** rico
**right** derecho; **to be right** tener razón
**romantic** romántico
**rose** rosa *f.*; rosado (*color*)
**rule** regla *f.*
**run** correr

## S

**sad** triste
**salad** ensalada *f.*
**salesman** vendedor *m.*
**sandwich** sandwich *m.*
**Saturday** sábado *m.*
**sausage** salchicha *f.*
**say** decir
**school** escuela *f.*; **in school** en la escuela; **school year** año escolar; **there's no school today**
no hay clases hoy
**science** ciencia *f.*; **science fiction** ciencia ficción *f.*
**season** estación *f.*
**seated** sentado
**second** segundo
**secretary** secretario *m.*, secretaria *f.*
**section** sección *f.*, parte *f.*
**see** ver; **I'll be seeing you, see you later** hasta la vista, hasta luego; **see you tomorrow** hasta mañana
**sell** vender
**September** septiembre
**serious** serio
**seven** siete
**seventeen** diez y siete
**seventy** setenta
**several** varios
**she** ella
**shirt** camisa *f.*
**shoe** zapato *m.*
**shoe store** zapatería *f.*
**shy** tímido
**sick** enfermo
**sing** cantar
**sister** hermana *f.*
**six** seis
**sixteen** diez y seis
**sixty** sesenta
**sky** esquiar
**skinny** flaco
**skirt** falda *f.*
**sleep** dormir
**sleepy: to be sleepy** tener sueño
**small** pequeño
**snow** nieve *f.*; **it snows, it's snowing** nieva
**snowball** bola de nieve *f.*
**snowman** figura de nieve *f.*
**so** tan, así; **so-so** así así, regular

**sock** calcetín *m.*, media *f.*
**soda** soda *f.*
**sofa** sofá *m.*
**some** unos, unas
**something** algo, alguna cosa
**son** hijo; **sons** *or* **son(s) and daughter(s)** los hijos
**sorry: I'm sorry** lo siento
**soup** sopa *f.*
**Spaniard** español *m.*, española *f.*
**Spanish** español *m.*; español
**speak** hablar
**special** especial
**splendid** magnífico
**sport** deporte *m.*
**spring** primavera *f.*
**station** estación *f.*
**steak** bistec *m.*
**still** todavía
**stocking** media *f.*
**store** tienda *f.*, almacén *m.* (*pl.* almacenes)
**street** calle *f.*
**strict** estricto
**strong** fuerte
**student** alumno *m.*, alumna *f.*; estudiante *m.&f.*
**study** estudiar
**stupid** estúpido
**suffer** sufrir
**suit** traje *m.*
**summer** verano *m.*
**sun** sol *m.*
**Sunday** domingo *m.*
**sunny: it's sunny** hace sol, hay sol
**superior** superior
**supermarket** supermercado *m.*
**supper** cena *f.*
**sweater** suéter *m.*

**T**

table mesa f.
take tomar
talk hablar
taxi taxi m.
teacher profesor m.,
   profesora f.
telephone teléfono m.;
   telephone operator
   telefonista m.&f.
television la televisión f.;
   to watch television
   mirar la televisión
tell decir
ten diez
tennis tenis m.
terrible terrible
terrific estupendo
test examen m.
thanks, thank you
   gracias; thanks very
   much muchas gracias
the el, la, los, las
theater teatro m.
their su, sus
then entonces
there allí; there is, there
   are hay
they ellos, ellas
thin flaco
thing cosa f.
think (of) pensar (en); I
   think yo pienso
thirsty: to be thirsty
   tener sed
third tercero
thirteen trece
thirty treinta
this este, esta
three tres
throat garganta f.
through por
throw lanzar
Thursday jueves m.
ticket billete m.

tie corbata f.
tiger tigre m.
time vez f. (pl. veces);
   (clocktime) hora f.; at
   what time? ¿a qué hora?;
   what time is it? ¿qué
   hora es?
times (X) por
tired cansado; to be tired
   estar cansado
to (in order to) para
today hoy
tomato tomate m.
tomorrow mañana
tongue lengua f.
town pueblo m.
train tren m.
transform transformar
transportation transporte
   m.
tree árbol m.
tropical tropical
true cierto; it's true es
   verdad, es cierto
truth verdad f.
Tuesday martes m.
twelve doce
twenty veinte
two dos

**U**

ugly feo
understand comprender
until hasta
use usar; used usado

**V**

vacation vacaciones f. pl.
vanilla vainilla f.; vanilla
   ice cream el helado de
   vainilla
vegetable legumbre f.
vegetarian vegetariano
very muy; the water is

very warm el agua está
muy caliente; I am very
warm tengo mucho calor;
it's very warm today
hoy hace mucho calor
visit visitar
vocabulary vocabulario
   m.

**W**

walk ir a pie, andar; take
   for a walk pasear
want desear, querer
warm caliente; to be
   warm estar caliente; ( =
   to feel warm) tener calor;
   (weather) hacer calor
watch mirar; (timepiece)
   reloj m.
water agua f. (el agua)
we nosotros, nosotras
wear llevar
weather tiempo m.; how's
   the weather? ¿qué tiempo hace?; the weather is
   bad hace mal tiempo;
   the weather is nice hace
   buen tiempo
Wednesday miércoles m.
week semana f.
welcome: you're welcome
   de nada
well bien
what? ¿qué?; at what
   time? ¿a qué hora?;
   what's your name?
   ¿cómo se llama Ud?,
   ¿cómo te llamas?
when cuando; when?
   ¿cuándo?
where donde; where?
   ¿dónde?; where (to)?
   ¿adónde?; where are you
   going? ¿adónde vas?,
   ¿adónde va Ud.?

which? ¿cúal?, ¿cuáles?
white blanco
who que; who? ¿quién?, ¿quiénes?
why? ¿por qué?
win ganar
wind viento *m.*
window ventana *f.*
windy: it is windy hace viento
winter invierno *m.*
wish desear, querer
with con; with me conmigo; with you contigo *(familiar)*
woman mujer *f.*
wonderful magnífico
work trabajo *m.;* trabajar; to work hard trabajar mucho
world mundo *m.*
worry preocuparse; don't worry no te preocupes
write escribir
wrong malo; to be wrong no tener razón

Y

year año *m.*
yellow amarillo
yes sí
you tú, usted (Ud.), ustedes (Uds.)
young joven *(pl.* jóvenes); young lady señorita *f.*
your tu, tus, su, sus

Z

zoo (parque) zoológico *m.*

# Grammatical Index

# Topical Index